Gospel Voices

Gospel Voices

ALEXANDER M. JACOBS

RESOURCE *Publications* • Eugene, Oregon

GOSPEL VOICES

Resource Publications
An Imprint of Wipf and Stock Publishers
199 W. 8th Ave., Suite 3
Eugene, OR 97401

www.wipfandstock.com

PAPERBACK ISBN: 978-1-6667-1745-7
HARDCOVER ISBN: 978-1-6667-1746-4
EBOOK ISBN: 978-1-6667-1747-1

07/14/21

Introduction

THROUGHOUT THE GOSPEL NARRATIVES, there are characters whose names and voices we recognize: Simon Peter: bold and brash; Thomas: disbelieving and skeptical; Herod cynical and brutal; Mary: humble and courageous. There are also many characters who have a voice but no name: the Canaanite woman: insistent and demanding; the blind beggar at Jericho: hopeful and pleading; the Roman Centurion: obedient and insightful. Woven into theses narratives are characters that can only be assumed and invented: the servants of the elite; the men and women of the crowds; the villagers who long for healing and justice; and the Pharisees who both criticize and concur. In this book I have tried to imagine what the many characters, named and invented, might say about how their lives were changed and challenged by coming face to face with Jesus of Nazareth.

As a teacher of the New Testament for many decades, I have sought to convince my students that these texts are not monological, but dialogical. The texts are one half of a conversation. Paul did not just lecture his congregations, he responded to their questions and concerns. The Gospel writers did not simply cut and paste from various traditional stories, they responded to the needs of various communities of faith. As a teacher, I sought to challenge my students to re-imagine the other half of the conversation that lies behind and beneath the narratives of the Gospels.

My intent in this book is to humanize the characters that are found in the Gospels. I have tried to portray them as flawed but faithful, realistic but ready to believe in miracles. I have sought to describe how they might think or imagine their responses and reactions to the power of God's work in the person of Jesus. I have tried to remain faithful to the various narratives as well as to the historical and cultural context of the story.

In the English translations of the Hebrew Scriptures, the name of "God" is often signified by JHWH (sometimes transliterated as "Jahweh").

However, since the name of "God" is not to be spoken by religious Jews, I have chosen to use the term "Adonai" for "God." In practice, whenever a Jewish man or woman is reading the Hebrew Scriptures and they come to the name of "God," they substitute "Adonai," which simply means "Lord." I have also changed the Greek/Latin name for "Jesus" to a more Hebraic "Yeshua." I have kept the names of characters and name places as they appear in the texts.

I am indebted to many for their encouragement, and especially to my wife Drusilla for her patience and care. I am deeply grateful to Isabelle Barry for her work as a copy editor.

Joseph

IF IT JUST WEREN'T so damned hot! This might be a good place to settle down. But Mary has her mind set on going back to Bethlehem. Other than this blasted heat, this is a good spot. There's water nearby, and a good marketplace—small, but good enough. The folks are friendly. There is even a synagogue—who would have thought it—a synagogue in Egypt. Pharoah would have crapped his pants, or whatever it was he wore. There is an even bigger synagogue in Alexandria. And a bunch of Torah thinkers who argue about the rules. Reminds me of my cousins in Nazareth. Maybe we should re-settle in Nazareth. There sure would be more work for a carpenter than there is here in the desert. But I like it here.

There is a trade route that goes through this village and I get lots of news of what's happening back in Judea. I haven't told Mary about the terrible news from Bethlehem. King Herod seems to have thrown one of his royal fits when he found us gone and those odd visitors from the East gone, too. Two weeks after our son was born, Herod sent his soldiers to Bethlehem and killed all the children under two years old. Just slaughtered them all. And some mothers and fathers, too. Blood everywhere. Good news for us. Bad news for the others. I had another of my dreams, and we managed to escape across the border into Egypt—and none too soon. Poor Mary. She just did not understand, and I did not have time to explain. The baby less than two weeks old and thrown onto a donkey in the middle of the night. No wonder she didn't understand. I didn't understand either.

Dreams are funny things. I never had many as a child. Oh, I had the usual dreams of any boy in Bethlehem. We all wanted to be like King David fighting lions and killing Goliath and chasing the Philistines into the sea. But I never had dreams, visions—with angels and voices. I was the last of my brothers to get married. I was too busy working, and I was never at ease with women, especially pretty young ones. Then there was Mary. Very young and sweet. It was her smile that got to me. I finally got the courage to ask her parents to marry her. They said "Yes." And so did Mary. Then came the first dream.

I knew enough about sex to know that women just don't get pregnant on their own. So, it crushed me when Mary came to me with this crazy story about an angel and her now being pregnant with a child from "you know who"—we're not supposed to use that name. Mad as I was, I couldn't just tell the world that my sweet Mary was a "you-know-what." I mean, I'm as religious as the next guy, but this was too much. So, I agreed to cancel the wedding and send her off quietly. Then, that night, I had this dream: an angel, I guess, appeared and told me not to give up on Mary but to marry her because she was pregnant by the Spirit of "you-know-who," and I was chosen to protect and care for the child. Well, I woke up in a cold sweat— I still do every time I remember that night. I never gave much power to dreams, but this was weird, I mean really weird. So, against my better judgment, I did agree to take Mary: dear, sweet, pregnant Mary. Turns out she is determined and critical, especially when I swear—which I do from time to time.

We never got formally married before the baby came. We, rather she, named him Yeshua because the angel told her he would be a savior, whatever that means. Then, about a week after he was born, the midwife had just left after changing the swaddling bands, and giving him a pinch on the butt to make him cry—she said it made him suck better. Who knows? I just didn't like him crying. Anyway, about a week after he was born, there was a ruckus down the street from our house. I opened the door to look out and there came these three men in fine, rich clothes, heading for our door. They stopped and asked, "Where is the baby born to be King of the Jews? We have come from King Herod, who told us he is to be born in Bethlehem. We have come to welcome him and to bring gifts in his honor." I almost swore at them, but I said, "I think he is in here. Our son—Yeshua." They came in and scared Mary half to death. She was nursing the baby and did not care to be disturbed. They bowed and knelt while she covered herself up and held the baby tight. Then I couldn't believe it. They knelt down and placed gifts in front of Mary—a leather bag of gold, a glass jar of myrrh, and a small chest of frankincense. The gifts were worth a fortune. I almost said "Holy . . . ! "But I just watched as they talked in a strange language and laughed and made clucking noises at the baby, who just wiggled and nuzzled for Mary's breast. If he only knew what was going on, he would have at least not farted. I made tea for them and they sat for an hour just looking at the baby sleep. Mary was very frightened but tried to smile and stay awake. Before they left, they asked me if I had seen his star in the heavens. I said, "No I hadn't." They took me outside and pointed to the dark sky in the East. "There!" they said. I gazed up and saw one star brighter than the rest. When I turned around, they were gone—pushing their way through the crowd to get to their camels. How was I going to explain this to the townsfolk? My rich cousins from Nazareth.

Well, the frankincense has almost run out. We used it as incense and as an ointment to prevent infection on our baby. It smelled so wonderful as it wafted through the house. We have never had it again since those first few weeks. The myrrh Mary set aside "for later in his life" she said. She was very mysterious about it. She began to cry, which she did a lot of in those first few weeks. Almost every time she looked at him, she had tears in her eyes. The gold has been used to keep us alive these past two years. Work has been sporadic in this village in Egypt.

When Jesus was almost two years old, I had another dream—my last one. I woke in the middle of the night with my heart beating fast. A voice I'd heard before said that King Herod was dead and we could return to Israel. A few days later I asked some in a caravan if it was true that King Herod had died. The merchants confirmed it was true It was now safe to return to Palestine, but I was nervous to go to Bethlehem since Herod's son now ruled there. I haven't told Mary yet. I know she will want to go back to her family in Bethlehem. I have to think about this in order to make them safe. I am afraid that Nazareth will be our new home.

Mary

I WOKE FROM A shallow sleep to Joseph's steady breathing. His broad back was turned toward me. Dear gentle Joseph—a good father and husband. I remembered how frightened he was when we first made love. He was so hesitant because of my, well, my unique experience. It's alright I said. "I am your wife and you are my husband." I know Yeshua is special, chosen, but I want him to have brothers and sisters, to know a family, to be, if possible, normal. I know I will never be "normal." and Yeshua will certainly never be "normal." I hope and pray that I will never again see or hear an angel. That night, I was both petrified and calm, chilled and warm. I could have said, "No," but I didn't. I said "Yes" and I am now glad I did. Yeshua is a wonderful child and Joseph is a wonderful man. I think I might be pregnant again. It has been almost two years since we fled from Bethlehem.

I quietly got out of bed and went outside to look at the heavens. I do this often. I try to look for Yeshua's star in the East. Joseph said that it had been there the night we received the three strangers. I am never quite sure which one is his. They all look so bright sometimes. What a strange visit. I was scared to death with a newborn and these three foreign men in rich clothes and strange language. They were very polite and wanted to worship the baby, of all things. I wouldn't let them hold him, though one wanted to. They sat still, smiling, talking quietly for almost an hour. Then they presented us with gifts of gold and frankincense and myrrh. I was stunned. I said thank you, but I doubt they understood. As they were leaving, they spoke with Joseph and pointed out the star. They said King Herod wanted to come and pay his respects, which was preposterous. We had just been in Jerusalem the week before to have Yeshua blessed and circumcised. Why didn't he find us then? When the strangers left, the villagers were asking Joseph all kinds of questions. I laughed when he told them they were his rich relatives from Nazareth.

Joseph took the gold and hid it. The frankincense we burned as incense and made a balm for stopping infection—both for Yeshua and me. I took the myrrh and put it away in my chest. I had a strange feeling that I would use it much later for a difficult time. Little did I know that a difficult time would come to us quickly. Two nights later, Joseph woke me and the baby in the middle of the night. "Quickly, pack up everything, get the baby. We have to leave." I didn't know what else to do, so I packed up, wrapped Jesus in sheepskin, for it was a cold winter. We loaded the donkey with as much as we could and set out for Egypt. We walked through the night and all of the next day until we found a small village that would take us in. We were given a small storage shed to live in. After we were settled and fed, I asked Joseph, "What happened? Why did we have to leave so suddenly?" He said that he had had another dream, and an angel had warned him to flee because King Herod wanted to kill Yeshua.

I could tell that Joseph was embarrassed that he had not only had a dream, but that he had believed it—how unmanly! He said that this wasn't his first dream. He said that he had had another one right after I told him I was pregnant. This was why he had agreed to marry me. He said he was afraid to go against what Adonai was doing in our lives, in the world. The angel told him not to be afraid. He seemed very relieved when I told him I had dreams as well. I had already told him of the angel appearing and telling me I would become pregnant with a child by the Holy Spirit. It amazed me that Joseph believed me. We soon learned from the caravans that his dream was true. Herod had sent his troops and killed all the children in Bethlehem aged two years or younger. I guess he was taking no chances.

Now another dream. Two nights ago, Joseph had a dream that Herod was dead and it was safe to return to Palestine. We are waiting to have the news confirmed before we return. Joseph has decided not to go back to Bethlehem but to go to Nazareth where he has family and can find work as a carpenter. I will miss my parents and cousins in Bethlehem, but it is not too far to visit. And it is best to keep our son safe. I am afraid that Nazareth will be our new home.

Herod

WHAT DID YOU EXPECT? I should have let him live? He had to die. Like all usurpers, he had to be done away with. Why couldn't they have said, "Where is the Messiah to be born?" Or "Where is the next prophet to be born?" Or anything but "Where is the King of the Jews to be born?" Did they not know who I am? Of course, they knew. They were mocking me. I almost had them killed right then and there. But I had a better idea.

I called my astrologers and my scribes and Torah experts. I asked them: "According to the prophets, where is the King of the Jews to be born?" They talked among themselves while I asked the three visitors, Magi I think they called themselves, how they knew of this event. They told me they had seen a particularly bright star rise in the sky and made calculations that led them here. My advisors came back and said, "He is to be born in Bethlehem, the city of David." I thought to myself, "What a joke. The King from that tiny town of nobodies." I thanked them and made out like I was really ecstatic. "Oh, please," I said, "Find him and then send word to me so that I might go and worship him too. I will send a few soldiers to guide you. It is not far; only a few miles to the South." I called three of my most trusted guards and told them, "Take the three Magi to Bethlehem and then stay and watch them closely. Don't let them out of your sight. When they find the house with the newborn child, mark it well and then bring them back to Jerusalem. I want to find out more from them."

So off they went. Well, those fool guards got drunk and lost the Magi. They never found them or the house with the child. Two days later they came back empty-handed. The most they could tell me was that the three strangers left by a different road—not the one back to Jerusalem, but off to the East toward the Jordan Valley. Gone! And so are those guards—dead and gone. I was furious. I called my advisors and the Captain of the Guard. I wanted to send them to Bethlehem and kill all the children. My advisors said, "All of them? That is too harsh, too unjust." I said, "Well then, all the children under age five." They looked shocked again and shook their heads. "All right. All the children under two years of age. That is my final decision!" I sent off the Captain to carry out my orders. I went to the window of the palace that looks out on the Gate to the South. I waited until I heard the horses snorting and watched them go off to make my kingdom safe again.

I know I have this dark side that comes out once in a while. Being a King is not easy. There is too much stress, too many decisions. And there are always enemies trying to challenge and even kill you. I have had to increase my personal bodyguard to 2,000 men. I have to be protected at all times. I have even had members of my own family oppose me and try to take away my power and crown. I had five wives and ten children and did not trust most of them. My dear second wife, Mariamne, was one who opposed me. In fact, her mother and both of our sons, Alexander and Aristobulus, were out to get me. They all had to die—eventually. I don't know what comes over me sometimes.

King of the Jews—indeed! I am the King of the Jews. God made ME the King of the Jews. Why then does he mock me? Why else would he have sent those three seers to me asking, "Where is he that is born King of the Jews?" I AM THE KING OF THE JEWS! God mocks me. I mock God!

I should have killed them all.

Eliud of Bethlehem

I AM STILL AWAKE. Every time I close my eyes, all I can see is blood. All I can hear is screaming, and babies crying, and . . . I don't think I will ever be able to sleep again. My brother Achim is the same, even though he did not see what I saw. Our sheep all are able to sleep—only the shepherds are sleepless. I pray that no dogs or lions come near. I pray—what a joke that is. How can anyone pray after what happened in Bethlehem yesterday?

We had just crossed the main road from Jerusalem. Our flock was heading into the field to the East for more grass. We heard the hoof-beats and looked North to see a cloud of dust rising into the morning sun. We knew it was either the Romans or the Palace Guards, so we hurried the sheep and switched the slow ones to get them into the fields quickly. Achim grabbed two young lambs and carried them into the middle of the flock. We stood on a rise and watched as the troops approached—Palace Guards. We wondered what Herod was up to this time. We were afraid to even imagine what his violent mind had caused him to send out the Guards.

We shooed the sheep further into the fields. These were the same fields we had settled in a week or more ago—the night it happened. I am not a religious person, but this was hard to deny or dismiss. It must have been after midnight when we heard a strange sound, like chanting or laughter or something at a wedding. We looked around and saw no one. Then the sky lit up like, like I don't know what. We were terrified, of course. The sheep started to bleat and cry and huddled in a circle. We tried to settle them, but it was no use. Then a voice, I swear a voice, said, "Go to Bethlehem and look for a newborn baby. He is the One. He is the One! He will bring Peace and Hope and Justice!" Then it was quiet again—still as before, except for the bleating sheep and our hearts in our heads.

I looked at Achim, who said, "What should we do? Should we go—to Bethlehem?" I said, "No. It makes no sense. We can't just leave the sheep."

Achim said, "I think we should go—go and look for the baby." I said, "Let me try to find Melchi. He can watch the sheep." "What if he's drunk?" "Let's hope he isn't." I ran off to look for Melchi, who sometimes helps out with the shearing and lambing. He was out near the road, and he was sober. I brought him back, and he agreed to watch the sheep.

Achim and I ran back to the road and hurried toward Bethlehem. We did not talk, only looked at each other with wide eyes. I wondered, "What if it's true? What if this baby is the One to change the world?" I looked over at Achim and he, too, was smiling. It was really easy to find them. Everyone seemed to know about the newborn baby. One woman said to us, "Oh, that one will make his mark on the world. He has a big voice already—kept us up most of the night with his crying. His poor parents are in for some tough times. The midwife said he was handsome but ornery—as if a little one could be ornery." We found the house and gently knocked and asked to see the baby. The father was hesitant but let us in. I remember that the light was strange; as if there was a lamp, yet there was no lamp. We looked for a few minutes, then thanked the mother and father. Achim said, as we were leaving, "We'll bring you a lamb's skin—to keep him warm. I'll wash it good." The father thanked us. Then we left. We couldn't stop smiling all the way back to the sheep pen.

No more smiles. Whatever hopes we had are gone—after what Herod did in Bethlehem. I am sure that the little newborn we saw that night is dead—chopped up—gone. Maybe even his parents are dead. We had seen the Palace Guards ride into Bethlehem, and shortly the first screams were heard. Within minutes, the screams and shouts grew louder and louder. I told Achim to wait with the sheep and I ran over the hills, just to the out-skirts of the village. I couldn't believe what I saw: the soldiers were slaugh-tering babies; killing them and tossing them into a pile. Some were holding back the towns-people, and some were breaking down doors and some were hauling off mothers and fathers, even hacking at them to keep them away from their children. I couldn't believe what I saw—and heard—and now can't forget. I wish we had never gone to Bethlehem that night. I wish we had never found the baby boy and his mother and father.

I walked back the Jerusalem Road, past Rachel's tomb. Like I said, I am not a religious person, but I remembered a line from one of the prophets: "Rachel weeping for her children, and she refused to be con-soled because they were no more." Some prophet also said, "None to comfort, none to comfort."

Melchior of Persia

SINCE WE WERE NOT used to traveling at night, we had to rely on two local traders to lead us to the Dead Sea. Once there, we could pick up the trade route to Petra in the Nabatean Kingdom. Our original plan was to return to Jerusalem. At least we would have had comfortable rooms and warm beds in Herod's palace. We were not counting on each of us hearing the same voice in our heads that warned us not to return but to flee. We had come out of the humble house in a state of ecstasy over finding the Star-Child, the one destined to be King of the Jews. We had all seen his star rise in the Eastern sky months before. We had written letters to each other to ask if we had all seen it and then we consulted all of our sacred texts: the Avesta and Vedic writings, and the Jewish Torah and Prophets. We even looked at Heraclitus, who thinks we are sinister and misguided; he and Herodotus were of no help. We look at the universe as a mystery. By that we mean it is not a problem to be solved, but to be approached with awe and wonder. The universe is also a witness: the great God reveals both purpose and events that will change the direction of history. We believe the universe is a gift, not a piece of property to be used and manipulated. We scan the heavens, looking for clues and signs of the great God's plan. We were not certain where the child was to be born, but we knew that it would happen soon. Our calculations did not include the fears of King Herod. We assumed that he, like us, would rejoice at the birth of a child who would bring peace and justice to the world. We were wrong.

Since we all lived in Persia, we met and traveled along the Silk Road, across Mesopotamia to Damascus, then down the Jordan Valley and up to Jerusalem. It was a long but not an arduous journey. Camels are not my favorite mode of travel, but they are plentiful and strong. We wanted to travel quickly, so we each had only two attendants: one for languages and one for protection. We were reminded how glad we were that Alexander had made

Greek the common language of his empire since it made travel and trade much easier. Changing Parthian silver for Roman silver was a problem, but we did not lose too much time or value in the haggling.

At night, when we spread out our star charts, the people who hosted us were fascinated and mystified by what we told them. We showed them how we could predict births and deaths, famines and wars by looking at how the stars and planets changed and re-aligned themselves. We debated whether to tell our hosts and fellow travelers why we were on this journey. We wanted so much to tell of the birth of the Star-Child and future King of the Jews who would bring peace and justice. However, we decided not to speak of it until we were certain—until we had seen the child for ourselves.

We arrived in Jerusalem in mid-afternoon, left our camels with our attendants, and entered the walled part of the city through the great Damascus Gate in the north. Since, among us three, I alone had been to Jerusalem, I suggested we make our way toward the Temple. Surely someone there would know the answer to our question. In the court of the Gentiles, we began asking people if they knew where the King of the Jews was to be born. They all looked frightened and turned away. One young man said that we should go to the palace and ask King Herod. He said it with a sneer and a laugh, then ran away. We were soon approached by some uniformed guards who asked us to follow them to the palace to meet with the king. We were glad to follow since this would surely give us our answer. They led us to the west and through a gate called Gennath. We stood on a wide-open pavement where we were told to wait. Soon a group of older men approached us and looked at us with disdain before they entered what we presumed to be the palace. In a few moments, a guard of high rank escorted us into the palace where we made our way to the chambers of Herod.

The King rose and greeted us warmly. He asked about our business in Jerusalem. I spoke up and said, "Where is the child to be born who is to be King of the Jews. We have seen his star rising in the east and have come to honor him." Herod could not hide his discomfort. His dark eyes moved back and forth from one of us to the other. Then he smiled or tried to smile. He called the group of elders we had seen enter before us and asked them our question: "Where is the King of the Jews to be born?" They talked among themselves and then said, "In Bethlehem of Judea: as it is written by the prophet: 'from you shall come forth a ruler who will govern my people Israel.'" He turned and said, "You have heard from my scribes and priests the answer to your question. Bethlehem is not far from here—only a few miles. I will have my guards escort you there." He then came close to us and stroked his beard and quietly said: "When you find the child, return to Jerusalem and tell me about him. I, too, would like to visit him and honor him. Will you do this?" We all agreed that we would return and let Herod know of the Star-Child.

While we were in Petra waiting to secure new camels and guides for the trip home, we learned the horrible news. Herod had sent soldiers to kill the children of Bethlehem. We were crushed; grief stricken. Surely the Star-child was dead. We should never have gone to Herod. How could we have known his fear and lust for power would drive him to such violence? We must have missed something in the stars. Or maybe in ourselves.

Leah of Nazareth

MY FAVORITE PLACE TO sit and think is here—on this cliff—looking over the plain of Megiddo. It is a secret place that only I know about. And I will never tell my sister Rachel. Maybe I will tell my brothers. It is too far to see Jerusalem, but I can almost see Har Megiddo, the mount on the other side of the valley. I like to imagine the many battles that have taken place on this plain. Some people even say that this is the place where Adonai's last battle will take place. I can see the heavenly host of angels swooping down to defeat the enemy of Adonai's people. I guess they would be the Romans. If it happens soon, I will have the perfect place to watch from this cliff. If my grandmother knew I was playing so close to the cliffs, she would probably tie me to my bed. She thinks it is too dangerous and even tells stories of how the villagers long ago would hurl trouble makers or public sinners off of these cliffs. I guess they thought it was a good way to make their place clean and holy. I think it is wrong and that God would not approve of such violence. But I am only a little girl.

Right now, I am looking to see if my cousin Joseph and his wife and son are coming across the valley. My father said that he got a message that Joseph was going to come to settle here with his wife, Mary, and their young son. Just what I need—another cousin to look after. Maybe Rachel can do it. She's older and thinks she's special just because she is named after the favorite wife in that story about Jacob. I overheard our mother and aunt saying that Mary was pregnant again so it will be a hard journey, especially if they have to walk. I guess they were living in Egypt, not Bethlehem where their son, Yeshua, was born. Nobody talks about why they had to move to Egypt. Whenever it comes up, everyone gets quiet and gives strange looks at each other. My aunt Naomi says, "Why are they coming here? They will just bring trouble. They caused big trouble in Bethlehem. They'll bring big trouble to Nazareth." My mother gives her a hard look and reminds her,

"Well, they are family so they will be welcome here." Then she points her finger at Naomi and says, loud enough for everyone to hear, "And there will be no gossip in this house." When my mother points her finger, "Watch out!" I can't wait to find out what the story is. I think I will just ask them when they get here.

Joseph is a carpenter and will work with another cousin at his shop. I think he would do better if he went to Sepphoris or Tiberias. There are lots of rich people in those cities. Nazareth is just a little town on a cliff with a tiny synagogue. I hear the synagogue in Sepphoris is huge—and really beautiful. Some elders think it is too much like the Roman temples, but I think they are just jealous. I hope Joseph knows how to work with stone, since that is what most people use to build their houses and shops. There is not much wood here unless you know some rich Romans or Phoenicians. My father said that they would have to live with another family until they can build a house or add some rooms onto another cousin's home.

Yeshua, Mary and Joseph's son, is two years old. His name means "the one who saves" or "rescues." My Aunt Naomi thinks they named him that just to show off. She says they think they are special and full of pride just because they come from Bethlehem, the city where King David was born. Our rabbi says Bethlehem is also the place where the Messiah will be born. I wonder if King David will come back to fight in Adonai's last battle. Yeshua is a good name: like Joshua, Moses' friend who was the leader of the army and a spy. I would like to be a spy. That would be exciting—sneaking around, finding out secrets and stuff.

Well, I don't see anybody coming up the road from the valley. I better get home to help with dinner or Rachel will cause trouble for me.

Hassan of Gaza

IT WAS AN UNUSUAL request; I admit. But I needed the money, so I agreed to go with them from Gaza to Nazareth. They asked me to be a kind of 'bodyguard' for a young family: a man, his wife, and two-year-old son. The parents seemed very nervous about travelling and asked me to avoid Bethlehem and Jerusalem, so I told them we would travel north along the coastline, then cut East when we got to Caesarea, through the Valley of Megiddo, then up to Nazareth. They seemed fine with that plan. The husband, Joseph, wanted a burro so his wife and son could ride. He was a carpenter and wished to trade his tools for a good animal. I asked my cousin Jethro, and he agreed to trade one of his burros for the tools. I think Jethro got the better of the exchange.

As we were packing the burro to travel, I noticed a familiar odor in one of the cloth bags. I asked, "Is that myrrh?" Mary looked surprised and embarrassed. She said, "Yes. It was a gift at Yeshua's birth." I told her I recognized it because Gaza was one of the major ports for exporting spices. The caravans came in from the East, from Petra and Dumah in the Nabatean Kingdom. One trader from Dumah always bragged he was from the family of Ishmael, Abraham's son, and so he had the best myrrh to trade. He said it was a family secret where he got it. I didn't believe him, but it was a great story. I said to Mary, "If you want to sell it, I can take it to my cousin who will give you the best price—not my uncle, he is too stingy." Mary said, "No thank you. I am saving it for a later time. I am afraid I will need it one day." She became teary-eyed and looked very sad when she said this. I tried to cheer her up by saying how lovely it will smell instead of that mangy old burro.

I was pretty sure that Mary was pregnant, so this would be a difficult journey. Also, they seemed to be overly protective of their son, who I guessed to be about three years old. We set out from Gaza early one morning. By noon, Yeshua was bored. He was more interested in running and playing than in sitting on a burro for hours at a time. I have younger brothers, so I know how busy they can be. I asked him if he knew about King David and he said, "Yes. I am going to be like him." His mother just shook her head and sighed. I grabbed him and put him on my shoulders and pretended he was King David riding into battle. We had run off the trail a short distance when I asked him if he knew the story of Goliath of Gath? He said, "No." I told him the story, and we acted it out. I explained Goliath was a giant: ten feet tall with hands as big as two lion's paws; he carried a spear as big as a tree trunk and a sword not even three men could lift. But David killed him with a small stone from a sling—"Popped him right between the eyes—wham! Like this." I grabbed my head and staggered away. I showed him how to wind up a sling and became very good at falling down dead in the dust: "But no throwing stones. Just pretend." I told him we would not pass far from Gath, the homeland of Goliath, and he begged to go see it. When I asked Joseph, he said, "No. We did not have time." Yeshua was very bright and seemed to know a lot of the old stories. I asked Joseph how he knew so much about our history. He smiled and said that he found it a good way to pass the time on the long nights in Egypt. Since there were few Jews in their village, they spent a lot of time together as a family. Joseph leaned in and quietly told me they did not tell him the story of Goliath because they did not want him to think that violence was a good way to solve problems: "We have already known too much violence." Then he changed the subject. He said he was looking for a new life in Nazareth; a more normal life with lots of cousins and relatives, peace and quiet, and family not just for Yeshua, his son, but for Mary, too.

Once we reached the major caravan route, we joined many others travelling north. At night there was lots of sharing of food and stories, so it was difficult to get Yeshua to settle down and sleep. The weather was pleasant with a cooling breeze from the wide sea. When we neared Caesarea, there were many more Roman soldiers marching along. We frequently had to stop and move off the road for them to pass. Yeshua was fascinated by their armor and weapons and the big horses of the officers. I warned him not to get too close to them because they dislike us. He frowned at me as if he knew what I was talking about. I suppose it is never too early to learn that we Jews are not free, even in our own land.

We turned inland through the plain of Megiddo and soon began the ascent to Nazareth. This was the hardest part of the journey, and Mary sometimes had to get off of the burro to walk up the steep trail. Joseph kept his arm around her while I tried to keep Yeshua from running ahead or off into the trees. When we were almost at the top, before Nazareth came into view, I noticed a young girl looking down at us from a cliff. I waved at her and she waved back. Then I heard her shout, "Are you Joseph and Mary?" We stopped and Joseph nodded his head. "I am your cousin Leah. We have been waiting for you." She disappeared only to come running down the path with a big smile on her face. "I am the first to see you. I will show you where we live. You must be Yeshua." She reached out and took Yeshua's hand and pulled him forward. "I'll take care of you."

Mary and Joseph

"WELL? WHAT DO YOU think?" said Joseph as they sat in their new surroundings.

"It's nice," Mary replied, almost asleep. She looked at her husband with tired, anxious eyes. "It will do."

"It is only for a while—until I can find another house, or we can add a few rooms to another house. My cousin said . . ." Joseph realized Mary was still missing Bethlehem and her own family. "I am sorry we could not go back to Bethlehem, but you know why."

Mary smiled and said, "It will be fine here. There are lots of children, and Yeshua has already found that a few dozen cousins are much more fun than just the two of us. Your families have been very gracious. There is much to do before the new baby comes—find a mid-wife, meet the rabbi, and get a new pair of sandals—mine are worn out from making me walk up that mountain." Mary gave a short laugh and then reached out for her husband's hand. "All of your relatives have been very kind—especially the women."

Joseph frowned, "All except Naomi. Be careful what you say to her. She is a gossip. She will pry into our life and then spread stories. She has already asked me why we didn't go back to Bethlehem and why we were away in Egypt for so long. She . . ."

Mary interrupted him, "Joseph, she is just curious. I hope she does not ask me if I believe in angels or miracles, or dreams. What should I tell her?" she teased. "Or do you want me to lie?"

Joseph laughed and knelt down to kiss her. They held each other and Mary said, "At least we know that this new baby is all yours."

Just then, Yeshua burst in the door, "Hassan found a snake and Uncle Benjamin killed it. I wanted to keep it, but he said it was from the Devil. Is that true? I don't believe it."

Joseph got up from the floor and said, "There is a story from the Torah. I will tell it to you some day." But Yeshua was out the door as fast as he had come in. He looked at Mary, who had lain back on the bed: "We are invited to share Shabbat with the family of Leah. They want you to light the candles."

"Do I have to? I am so tired."

"It is a great honor, and they just want to make sure you are really Jewish," Joseph smiled and then covered Mary with a blanket.

Naomi of Nazareth

"SUCH A FUSS! SUCH a fuss!" Naomi said to herself. "Like we have never had distant relatives come to Nazareth before." She was cooking food for the next day and had to finish before sundown. "Tomorrow is Shabbat and I will have a chance to sit and talk with Mary and find out more about her and Joseph and that little boy, Yeshua. What a presumptuous name," she thought as she pondered how to approach her cousin's wife. "There is something strange going on here: a sudden marriage with no engagement; no family celebration; then an unexplained leaving of Bethlehem, and a few years in Egypt. They were lucky to get out when they did, what with Herod on one of his crazy rampages—killing all the children in the village. I wonder how they knew to leave when they did—something strange, indeed."

I am married to one of Joseph's cousins, Zephaniah, who works as a stonecutter. He also owns a small portion of an olive grove. People sometimes look at me funny because I walk with a limp as the result of an accident many years before. As a young woman, I had been trying to help my husband with a load of stone when the cart collapsed and broke my leg. It confined me to the house for many months, which was when I started to take an interest in what everyone else in the village was doing, or not doing. We have two children: a boy of twelve and a girl of eight. I have a reputation as one of the best cooks in Nazareth, and I especially enjoyed cooking and baking with the other younger women in the village. It's a time to hear all the family gossip. I am glad when the older aunts and grandmothers don't join us because they are very critical of our storytelling and go on about "bearing false witness," and not repeating what we're not sure is the truth. What fun is that!

I have an eye on my niece Leah as a match for our son Ari. Leah is beautiful, but far too independent. She will go off by herself and wander in the woods and wild places. Her grandmother told me she is afraid she goes too close to the cliffs and may someday fall over the edge and kill herself. I will have to teach Ari how to be a strong man and keep her in her place. His father won't be able to do that. Now this Mary, too, seems to be an independent type. I will have to find out more about her and how she thinks and behaves. And I must find out about their marriage and time in Bethlehem. She probably thinks she is better than us since she comes from King David's hometown. Well, being from the Galilee is far better than being from the southern part of Israel. It is so hot and dusty down there. We are much freer up here in the north and don't have to bow down to those Jerusalem priests. They are all in league with the Romans, anyway. Those Romans and all their taxes. I hope the young men go join the Zealots and fight those Romans again. But not Ari—he is too special and must learn his father's trade and marry Leah.

Mary and Joseph

"WHAT DO YOU WANT to name your son?" Mary asked Joseph as he stared mutely at his newborn.

"What? What did you say?" Joseph replied. He was still amazed at his second son. "He has all that black hair. And a funny nose." "It's your nose—not mine," Mary laughed. "I was thinking of naming him Gershom, after Moses' first son. Remember? He said, "'I have been a sojourner in a foreign land.' And this little one has done a lot of travelling lately. What do you think? What would you name him?"

"I was thinking of Yaakov I want him to be strong enough to wrestle with angels."

"Don't you think one 'angel-wrestler' is enough? I mean, Yeshua is already wrestling with everyone. But Yaakov will be fine a good name. I just hope people don't start calling him 'Jacobus'—as though he were a Roman."

"I hope he can now be settled down. I hope we, too, can be settled for a while. I know this is not like Bethlehem where we had our own house, but it will get better after I can find more work. Samuel said there is work for boat builders in Capernaum, but I have never built a boat and I do not want to move again. Hassan says he knows a merchant who can get some cedar from the north, but it is still expensive and who could afford to buy what I might make."

"Hassan is still in Nazareth? I thought he would have gone back to Gaza by now."

"I guess you have not heard. He has his eye on Rachel, one of the young women of the village. She is quite beautiful, but still very young. He says he can wait, and he also wants to show everyone in Nazareth what a good worker he is. He would make a good rabbi with his story-telling ability. But I think the older folks would not appreciate how he adds a lot of, shall we say, extra details to the stories. He has all the children running after him, wanting to hear the David and Goliath story again and again. He has Goliath up to twelve feet tall and his spear the size of a tree."

"They say that Capernaum is stunning, and the Sea of Kinneret is delightful and full of fish. But I do not want to move again for quite a while. Maybe when Yeshua is grown we can think about moving again."

Joseph knelt by the bed and smiled at his new son. He then touched Mary's head and stroked her hair. "I never thought I would be this happy." He took a deep breath and got to his feet. "But now I have to help Zephaniah with a load of stone. Someone is adding another room to their house. I am very jealous."

"Soon we will have our own house again," said Mary. "And now I am going to sleep while Yaakov is sleeping. Please take Yeshua with you so he won't come and wake us." As Joseph was at the door, Mary called out, "And talk to the rabbi about Yaakov's circumcision. Or Naomi will tell everyone what terrible parents we are." She smiled and Joseph shook his head and laughed.

Eleazar the Scribe of Jerusalem

HE WAS BY FAR the most unusual young man I have ever met. It was not just his grasp of the Torah and the stories of the people and patriarchs, but his intensity was disturbing, to say the least. "His poor parents" was all I could think of when they finally showed up at the Temple. He had been with us for several days and did not seem afraid in the least. They were distraught and angry, and I am sure, happy all at the same time. I introduced myself and told them that their son had been staying with me and my family until they arrived. His mother smothered him with her arms and wept into his hair. His father thanked me, but I saw a deep emotion of fear and rage beneath his calm. I tried to let him know he had a remarkable and very gifted son, but he did not hear me, I am afraid. "Please do not strike him," I said to Yeshua's father. He frowned and said, "You mean, 'Spare the rod and spoil the child' is not good advice?" I said, "Even better advice is 'Your rod and your staff they comfort me.'"

It all began the day after Passover. This young man, Yeshua of Nazareth, maybe twelve or thirteen years old, showed up in the Temple by himself. He simply sat and listened to us, the Scribes and Sadducees, talking and debating about the Torah. I think we were talking about what to do with leftover bread and food from the Passover feast in a family's home—Eat it? Bury it? Burn it? He spoke up, which in itself was startling, and said, "Why not give it to the poor?" No one had ever interrupted our conversations before. We were all startled—and silent. Then Joachim said, "We should not give it to the poor because we could not know if they were 'clean' or had washed their hands." Most of us agreed with him, but Yeshua said, "I would give it to the poor because they are hungry." No one spoke, so he continued: "In the Torah, are we not told that Moses said that a family that was too poor to have its own lamb or goat should share with another family?" Ebenezer frowned and said, "The command is for a family that is too small, not too poor." Yeshua thought for a moment and then replied, "Maybe the word could mean that the family's wealth is too small—not just its size." I had to smile as I watched Ebenezer fidget in his seat. I stroked my beard and said, "The boy has a point. He could be right. We should look again at the text before we decide. At any rate, I think sharing with the poor is a good idea." It amazed me that most of the men agreed with me.

When our discussions were over, I wondered where his parents were and watched as he seemed to be lost in thought. I asked him if his parents knew he was in the Temple. They might worry. He said, "They probably think I am with my cousins. We are all from Nazareth—in the Galilee. They will come for me soon. I will just wait here until they find me." I decided to wait with him.

"Where did you learn so much about the Torah and our traditions?" I asked him. "My mother and father have always told me stories. When I was very young, we lived in Egypt for a few years. There wasn't much to do at night, so they told stories and made me learn about Passover and other traditions. In my village of Nazareth, there is Rabbi Matthias. He gathers all the young boys at the synagogue every week and teaches us to read the Torah. At least he tries to gather us together. Many of them have to help their fathers, and some just don't want to learn. My parents insist I attend and learn. I can read the Torah pretty well, but Isaiah is my favorite." "Why is that?" I asked. He thought for a moment: "I think because he talks so much about God doing new things—not the same old stuff. And he wants us to look for hope even when life is hard and we don't get our way, or when things go wrong." He suddenly smiled and laughed and said, "And then there is Hassan." "And who is Hassan?" I asked. "Oh, he is from Gaza, but he has been living in Nazareth for many years. He even married a woman from Nazareth. When my family left Egypt, we did not go back to Bethlehem, where my parents lived and got married. They decided to move to Nazareth. Hassan helped us travel and found a good donkey. He knew the way since he had traveled with some caravans with his brothers. Hassan loves to tell stories—he should have been a rabbi. His favorite story is David and Goliath. Did you know Goliath was twelve feet tall? At least according to Hassan, he was—I don't think so. I think Hassan helped me appreciate a good story. Sometimes I like to make up stories myself. I only tell my parents—never the rabbi. He might think I was being, well, disrespectful, you know, of tradition. My father is a carpenter, and he likes me to tell him stories while he is working on stuff. My mother just smiles and laughs, even when I am trying to be serious. Maybe I will be a rabbi someday." I believe you will be, I said to myself—I believe you will be a rabbi.

Joseph

I DID NOT EXPECT him to burst into tears when we finally found him. Probably a good thing since I was so angry, I might have struck him. Who does he think he is! Leaving us to search for him for two days! His poor mother! Mary was frantic. All I could do was hope he had not been grabbed off the street by some Phoenicians and sold to a caravan—or by Romans—what horrid stories I have heard.

We were out of ideas of where to look when we wandered into the outer courts of the Temple. And there he was—sitting with some old men— like he belonged with them. Mary screamed, "Yeshua!" and he jumped up and began to cry. Then he ran to her, and she collapsed on the ground as she hugged him. I just stood back and glared at him. He saw my look and buried his head in Mary's shawl. Who does he think he is! I wanted to break something so I wouldn't break him.

As I was trying to settle myself, an old man approached me. "You must be Joseph, the boy's father," he said. I could not speak, so nodded my head. "I am Eleazar, a Scribe in the Temple. Yeshua, your son, has been staying with me and my family for these past two days. He is a remarkable young man—a very disobedient young man—but remarkable just the same." I nodded again. "His poor mother has been sick and sleepless. She was sure we had lost him for good. Thank you for your kindness. I hope I can forgive him. I hope I can forgive myself. We thought he was with the rest of our family—with his cousins. We had traveled all day and did not look for him until suppertime. When we realized he was lost, we walked most of the night to get back to Jerusalem. Hassan, one of our friends, came with us. The soldiers would not let us into the city until we convinced them we were telling the truth—that we had lost our son. Thank you for your kindness." Then I, too, began to cry. Eleazar put his hand on my head and blessed me. He said, "He will bring great gifts to his people—and, I fear, great turmoil,"—and I thought to myself, "Just as he has brought turmoil to me and his mother."

Hassan of Gaza

WHEN THEY FINALLY FOUND Yeshua in the Temple, I just stood at a distance, hoping that Joseph would not strike his son. One of the Scribes was speaking to him as they watched Mary cry over her son. I felt a little guilty since Yeshua had told me he wanted to spend time in the Temple when we were in Jerusalem. He thought it would be fun to explore the different places and even talk to some priests and scholars. I told him he needed to be careful not to break any rules or go somewhere that was forbidden. "You think we have rules in Nazareth," I told him, "You have no idea how many rules there are in Jerusalem. And the Temple is the place with the most rules in the world. Except maybe in my house—you know how Rachel's mother is." I wish I had not tried to make light of the whole visit to Jerusalem. Now he was in real trouble. Yeshua is the oldest son of the family and is supposed to set an example. His brother Jacob will never let him forget this mistake.

Before we set out again for Nazareth, the elderly Scribe supplied us with some food and water. He offered a donkey, but Joseph would not accept. He also invited Yeshua's family to visit him on their next trip to Jerusalem. Joseph glared at his son and said, "If there is a next trip." Mary held her son close and tried to smile at her husband, but to no avail. So, we set out for Nazareth only no one talked for hours. We made it as far as Mount Gerizim before we found a place to rest. Fortunately, the weather was dry and warm. We ate our dinner in silence, then Mary and Joseph fell asleep.

Yeshua wanted to tell me all about his time in the Temple, but I told him to wait a day or two, hoping things would settle down in his family. He knew he was in for a rough time at home and in the town. I found it ironic that he was so intrigued with and excited about the Temple—Herod's Temple. He must have heard about how horrible Herod was, and especially about his massacre of the children in Bethlehem. After all, he had been born there and barely escaped with his own life. I wonder if Mary and

Joseph have ever told him about this horrific event and how they escaped to Egypt. I still wonder about that, since that is the reason that we met in the first place. If they had not been looking to move back to Palestine, we never would have met and I never would have helped them find a new home in Nazareth, and I never would have met Rachel. Like some prophet said, "Adonai works in mysterious ways." But now the only mystery is what this creator of ours is going to do with this brilliant, bull-headed, rebel named Yeshua. I think I need to find him a girlfriend.

Leah of Nazareth

MY COUSIN JOSEPH WAS beside himself because of his eldest son, Yeshua. He had no complaints about his work in the carpentry shop. His son was quick to learn the trade, and he worked hard on whatever job Joseph gave him to do. But he could not understand why Yeshua was always day-dreaming and asking questions about everything. Joseph said he often felt stupid because he didn't have answers to a lot of his questions, especially questions about the Torah or traditions or evil or injustice. Yesterday he said, "Why doesn't he ask me about how to pick out a good donkey, or which wood is best for door frames, or girls—he never asks me about girls." Joseph still has not gotten over the incident in Jerusalem at Passover. "You are his favorite cousin," Joseph told me. "Why don't YOU talk to him?" I promised I would.

On the next Sabbath, I asked Yeshua to go for a walk with me instead of taking the usual afternoon rest. I thought I would show him my secret spot near the cliffs on the south edge of the village. I had not been there for several years, since I was married and now had a two-year-old child. We walked on the main road out of Nazareth and I was glad it was Sabbath so no one else was in sight. I looked closely for the big rock that marked the place to turn into the forest. "This way," I said suddenly, almost pushing him to the right behind the rock. "Where are we going?" Yeshua asked. "It's a secret," I said with a smile. He smiled back, like a good co-conspirator.

We made our way through the trees and scrub grass climbing down across a few large stone outcroppings finally arriving at the open spot with the view of the plain of Megiddo. Yeshua just stood and stared for a few moments. Then he exhaled with a whistle and said, "This is amazing. It is like a vision of, of, of the future." I told him that this was my own secret place where I used to come as a child. "I came here to watch for you and your parents when you first came to Nazareth. In fact, I was the first one to see you coming across the plain and up the steep path." He smiled at this and reached for my hand. "Even my family does not know of this place, so you have to promise to keep it a secret." "Oh, I will," he said. "I won't tell anyone about it." He dropped my hand and walked to the edge of the cliff and looked down. "Be careful!" I spoke. "It is a long way to the bottom. They say that in the old days the villagers would throw blasphemers off this cliff to their death. I don't know if it is true or not. But it would be a terrible way to die." "Is there a way to escape if you were trapped here—maybe by an angry mob?" he asked with a playful smile. "Actually, there is," I said. "If you were to jump off to the far left, there is a shelf about ten feet down. If you land on it, there is a path that leads back to the main road. I tried it once when I was about your age."

I then said to Yeshua, "Come! Sit here on this rock with me." He turned and gave me a look like, "Oh no! Here comes the lecture!" He came and sat next to me and I said, "Your parents worry about you. After that episode in Jerusalem, they are not sure what to think about your behavior—that is, your thinking and always asking questions, and never being satisfied with the simple, traditional answers. I hear that even the rabbi finds you too, well, too inquisitive. My nephew Reuben calls you a 'know-it-all' but I think he is just jealous that you are so far ahead of him in learning the Torah lessons. And your father is concerned that you don't seem to show any interest in—well—in girls." I paused and looked at him. He was looking at his sandals and rubbing a stone in his hands.

Yeshua threw the stone over the cliff and waited to hear it bounce off of a rock. He looked out toward Har Megiddo and said, "Do you really think this will be the place of the last battle between good and evil?" Then, without letting me answer, he said, "I don't. I don't think Adonai is interested in battles and fighting and warfare. I think he is much more interested in forgiveness—and love—and mercy." I smiled and put my arm around his shoulder. "I do, too," I said. "But you will have to find a way to stop worrying your parents, and to be more . . ." "More normal?" he said. I just smiled. "So, I have to get a girlfriend?" he asked. "That would help," I said. "How about Miriam? She's cute. Or Hannah. I hear she's a wonderful cook." He kicked the stones at his feet and said, "OK. I'll try." Then he looked up at me and asked, "Do you think there will ever be another prophet? Like Amos? Or Isaiah?" I looked into the distance and replied, "Maybe. Just maybe there will be."

Joseph

IF WE HAD MOVED to Capernaum, this never would have happened. I could still work and care for my family. Now I can hardly walk, let alone carry stone or lift things. Poor Mary has to do a lot more. It's a good thing I have three sons and two daughters to help with the work and to keep the carpentry business going. Yaakov is married with one child, and he works the hardest. Elizabeth is also married, but no children—yet. She helps Mary with the cooking and gardening. But she will soon need to pay more attention to her own family. Joseph is to marry in the Spring—a young woman from Nain. And he may decide to move in with her family. Tirzah is too young, but is even now the best baker in the village. I am very proud of her—of all my children, really.

I am most concerned about Yeshua. He is the eldest but is still single—and does not seem to be interested in marriage. He is very handsome and all the young women look at him and find ways to be near him, when it is appropriate—which, with all the Pharisees and gossips in the village, is not very often. He works hard with his brothers and is always ready to help any of the neighbors with whatever they ask. I think they take advantage of his good nature, but he just smiles and says, "They might be angels in need—and we wouldn't want to offend them." I often catch him gazing off into the sky. He says he is praying, but I think he is thinking too much. Maybe he is having visions—I don't know.

He spends a great deal of time with an elderly rabbi in Capernaum. He tells me some stories that he has heard from him. He calls them 'parables'—about wise and foolish people, servants and kings, rich and poor people who do puzzling things. I don't always understand them—but I listen—before I try to change the subject to work or marriage or something practical. He has said that he wants to be a rabbi, and I tell him he is too young. "You must be older, and a gray beard helps." We laugh and then I tell him he is too easygoing, not strict enough. He then gets serious and looks away. Sometimes he says that Adonai must have a sense of humor. Just look at the donkeys and camels that we depend on. And then look at how he loves us, despite our foolishness and decisions. I have to admit that he is right about that.

He is a good son. He was with me when the accident happened. We were unloading some heavy stone blocks from a cart when it tipped over and one block fell on my left leg. Yeshua tried to move it off of me, but it was too heavy. He called for help, then wedged a board under the stone to prevent it from moving anymore and doing more damage to the leg. It took three men to lift the stone. When they pulled me out, it was clear that my lower leg and foot had been crushed beyond repair. As they carried me to the physician, I tried to make light of it. I said to Yeshua, "It's a good thing I don't want to become a priest—no cripples allowed." He nodded and said, "I told you Adonai has a sense of humor." Neither of us laughed though, because my accident was far too serious.

Ruth of Nazareth

I CAN'T BELIEVE I burned the bread again this morning. My mother, Naomi, was furious—again. This time I had no ready excuse. The last time I was able to blame my older brother for teasing me and making me forget to watch bread closely. He was teasing me, though I never told my mother what about. He said that I was in love with Yeshua and was always looking for ways to run into him in the market or after synagogue. This time when the bread burned, I could not think of anything, so I just cried. This made my brother laugh even harder, and whisper he was going to tell our father that I was chasing after Yeshua and bringing embarrassment to the family.

It is true—I burned the bread—twice. It is also true that I am in love with Yeshua. He is so kind and gentle. And handsome, especially when he smiles. But he smiles at everyone. And he is kind to everyone. I get jealous because I want him to pay more attention to me. I know that is wrong and I wish I could feel otherwise—but I can't. I love to hear him tell stories to the young children after the synagogue gatherings. I am always the oldest person listening, and I try to pretend to be busy with something else, as I stand at the edge of the circle. But I think he has noticed that I am listening to his stories, and he even looks right at me so I have to look away and hope he does not see me blush. He always connects his stories to the Torah or traditions and encourages the children to use their imagination and find new meanings. Some elders are not at all pleased with his "parables," as he calls them. I think they are wonderful. I could listen to him all day—and all night, for that matter.

I have also come to realize that there is another stumbling block when it comes to Yeshua—my mother. She does not like his mother, Mary. She keeps saying that there is something about her that isn't right, that there is a secret somewhere in her past that will come out some day and it will not be good for anyone. She thinks Joseph knows the secret, but is bound not to tell. I think they are both very nice. And they surely love each other very much. They have a wonderful family with five children, and they have become a big part of our village and our synagogue. I think my mother just doesn't like anyone from southern Israel. It is, however, a shame about Joseph's accident and he is very lame since it happened. I guess this means that Yeshua will have to be the main provider for the family. I think he will need a wonderful wife to help him. I just can't burn the bread ever again. Or maybe if I keep burning the bread, my mother will want to marry me off sooner—and I have just the husband in mind.

Ben Sirach of Capernaum

EVERY TIME I OPEN my eyes, I expect to see the gray smoke of Sheol. But again, there is light. Not the dark shades of everlasting night, but the shimmering glare of Gennesaret. I say the Hallel Psalms under my breath and swing my ancient, crippled feet to the floor. I wait for a moment before I try to stand. I call out for Binyamin and he quickly appears at the door—smiling as always. I keep wondering what he is so happy about—which girl is it this week. He pulls the nightshirt over my head and then straightens my hair with a laugh. "At least I still have some hair," I say, trying to be gruff with him. "Yes! Yes! And it is not even white yet," he says with mock dignity. He holds up two tunics: "The brown one or the other brown one?" I frown and point at one or the other. "Whichever makes me look more scholarly," I say with my chin out. "Oh, then this one will do fine," and he pulls it over my head and holds the sleeves for my arms. "Is Yeshua coming again today?" he asks. "I suppose so," I reply. "He will probably have another dream or vision to ask me about." "Your neighbor, Simon, was asking about him. I believe he is looking for another fisherman to help with his business." "Oh, Yeshua is a carpenter. I doubt he knows anything about fishing. Probably can't swim either." We both laugh.

It has been almost a year since Yeshua started coming to talk with me. We met by accident on a Sabbath. He had come from Nazareth to deliver some door frames which needed fitting. It took him longer than expected and then he realized he could not return to Nazareth before sundown, so he stayed in Capernaum. After prayers at the synagogue, I realized he had no place to stay, so I invited him to my home. I live alone, so it was no problem. We got to talking, and I realized he was well versed in Torah and the Prophets and had some interesting and unusual insights. He was an observant Jew, but thought that there were too many restrictions that might hinder doing good and showing care for a neighbor. He also thinks that we are far too worried about purity than about mercy and hospitality. I asked him once if he would allow a Roman soldier into his house. He said, "Sure. As long as he didn't eat too much." We both chuckled, but he knew I was serious about keeping company with foreigners and those who have committed violence against our people. I said, "So you don't put much stock in Leviticus then." He pondered a few moments and then said, "How will we convince the Romans that Adonai is for all people if we do not first show them that our homes are places of hospitality and welcome?" "Maybe our Adonai is not for all people, but only for a chosen few?" "Why then would Adonai create so many different people if he did not intend to love them all?" "But our Scripture says that we alone are the chosen ones." "Yes, but chosen to do what? Not to be a blessing only to ourselves. We are children of Abraham to be a blessing to all the nations—even Romans." I sighed and shook my head: "You are going to get yourself in a lot of trouble with that kind of thinking." He looked into the distance and said, "It won't be the thinking, but the acting that will get me into trouble." I said, "I am tired. Let's get some sleep," knowing full well I would not sleep much that night.

Mary

BY THE TIME YESHUA had returned from Capernaum, Joseph was delirious. The infection in his leg had returned days before, and he had told no one. Maybe we should have agreed to the amputation. Who knows? I found him writhing in pain when I came back from the garden with vegetables for dinner. He was crying and beating the floor. I got him into bed, pulled off the dressing, and saw that the wound was festering and smelled horribly—like death itself. I called for Yaakov to run for the physician—and the rabbi. I bathed Joseph's leg and tried to apply some salve, but he screamed and fought me, so I waited for his children to hold him down. I knew it was no use, but I wanted to do everything I could. I prayed, and I prayed, and I prayed. I bargained with Adonai, like Sarah, who prayed that if her son Isaac returned from Mount Moriah unharmed, she would never doubt again. I told Adonai that I would never again question why my son Yeshua would have to do whatever it was that Adonai wanted him to do. I asked for Adonai to spare Joseph and he could have Yeshua.

As I watched Yeshua sit with his father intoning a Psalm: "My God! My God! Why have you forsaken me? Why are you so far from me?" I could only remember the night Adonai had called out to me through an angel. I would have a son. As crazy as that sounded, I was strangely at peace. Over the years, I have often felt overwhelmed and not at peace. What does Adonai want from us? What will happen to this child of mine? Is he really mine? My first-born son? If not mine, then whose? What will happen to us when Joseph dies? Will Adonai have a change of mind and let Yeshua marry and become the head of the family like other Jewish sons? So, I continued to bargain. But to no use. Joseph died in the evening, surrounded by his family and the rabbi. We all wailed to let the rest of the people of Nazareth know Joseph was dead. Outside of our home, the people also began to wail. Only Yeshua was not wailing because his tears of grief were too great.

Binyamin of Capernaum

TODAY BROUGHT MIXED EMOTIONS—STRONG feelings about loss and hope. Rabbi Ben Sirach had died last week. Today was the day I had to travel to Nazareth to invite Yeshua ben Joseph to become our rabbi in Capernaum. I remember the night that Rabbi Ben Sirach had first suggested this arrangement to Yeshua. They had been studying the call of Jeremiah and the prophet's reluctance to consider the call because he was still very young. Yeshua had said that in many circles my young age is not considered the proper age for a rabbi. Ben Sirach had countered, "But where is that stated in Scripture? Remember Jeremiah?" Yeshua had laughed and said, "Now you sound like me." "You must be a wonderful influence on an old man," Rabbi continued. "Adonai got angry with Jeremiah: 'Don't say 'I am just a boy.'' I can choose whomever I want. And I choose you." Yeshua smiled and said, "And then Jeremiah asks, 'What will I say? They won't listen to such a young person.'" Rabbi quoted, "'You shall go to whomever I send you and you shall speak whatever I command you.'" Yeshua shook his head and said, "And we all know how that turned out—doomsday prophet, social outcast, thrown in a pit, laughed at—some fun." Then Rabbi said, "Just remember the keywords: 'Don't be afraid of them. I am with you to deliver you.'" Yeshua smiled and said, "That's what my father Joseph used to say to me: 'Don't be afraid.' He said he learned that from my mother." They sat in silence for a time and then Yeshua said, "OK. I will try it. I have already met all the villagers and even spoken in your synagogue so it won't come as a complete surprise."

Now I have to go and tell him that another important man in his life has died. He has just mourned his father, and now his teacher. I hope I can do this with some comforting words and some dignity. Now I am sounding like Jeremiah. Well, the good news is that Rabbi Ben Sirach has left Yeshua both his house and his library. There is plenty of room for him and his mother, if she wants to move to Capernaum. There is even a small room for a helper like me. And I really don't eat much, and I know all the folks in the village. I can even teach him how to fish—and swim. And there are some accomplished young women in Capernaum, should he be looking for a wife. Now I sound like my aunt Milcah. Well, it is time to go. It is not a long journey to Nazareth, but it is all uphill. May Adonai be with me in my journey.

Simon of Capernaum

IT WAS THE DAMNEDEST thing I had ever seen. I would not have believed it if I had not been there myself. We had just come in from a long day of fishing. A crowd was waiting for us on the beach, so Andrew began selling fish. James and John started cleaning the boats and the nets. I have given up letting James and John try to sell fish since they always get into an argument with the customers, and even a fight or two. I went home to wash up for supper. When I arrived, I was told that my mother-in-law was sick with a fever. I was worried about her, but also upset because the new rabbi was coming to eat with us. I was about to ask our neighbor's son to go and tell Rabbi Yeshua not to come when he turned up at the door. I apologized for smelling like fish and then told him my wife's mother was ill and maybe he should come another day. He smiled and asked, "Where is your mother-in-law?" I pointed to the back room of the house, walked over and pulled aside the curtain. He went in and sat down next to her on the bed. Then he took her hand in his, put his other hand on her head, and prayed. In minutes, her eyes opened,, she sat up, laughed softly, swung her feet to the floor and got up. "I think I ought to help get supper ready," she said, and shuffled off to the kitchen with my wife. Everyone just looked stunned. Rabbi Yeshua said, "I hope we are having fish for supper. I hear there are at least two wonderful cooks in your family."

While I was washing the fish smell away, our neighbor and his wife came up and said, "What just happened? We were with your wife, trying to comfort her mother when this young man came in and sat next to her and prayed and the next thing we knew, your mother-in-law is cooking supper." We looked at each other in amazement. I said, "I don't know what to say. He is the new rabbi, and . . ." and I just shrugged, "Some kind of miracle." My neighbors then said, "Maybe he can help Levi's father—the one who keeps crying out and yelling at people—even in the synagogue." They ran off to find him. I finished washing and went in to wait for Andrew and entertain our guest, mumbling, "We are out of wine. Maybe he can do something about that too."

While we were waiting for supper, Rabbi Yeshua and I began to talk and I learned that his mother would join him soon." "What, no wife?" I joked. "There are plenty of good women in Capernaum. And they are all wonderful cooks like my wife." He laughed and said, "No. I am not married—at least not yet. I am not sure I would be a good husband since I, well, I don't know what the future holds for me." He paused and then continued, "Before I begin as rabbi, I want to meet this new preacher, John—the one who is baptizing in the Jordan down near Jerusalem." I huffed and said, "I've heard about him. Sounds kind of wild to me. And he should come and do his baptizing here in Galilee. Our Jordan is much cleaner than down near Jerusalem. Too much money and corruption—and too many of those damned Romans—pardon my language." Yeshua laughed and then said, "Maybe John thinks they are more in need of healing. You know the old saying, 'It is not the healthy that need a physician, but only the sick.'" I agreed and then said, "I think supper is ready. Hope you are hungry."

Binyamin of Capernaum

WHAT I THOUGHT WAS going to be a smooth transition turned out to be anything but. Rabbi Yeshua had been with us in Capernaum for only a few weeks when he decided he needed to go into the wilderness for a few days to pray and reflect. But before he did that, he was going to find this new preacher, John, and be baptized. He thought it would be a good new beginning. I am not so sure. Some are calling John a prophet; some are calling him a fraud; some are calling him a Zealot; others are even calling him the Messiah. I just know that he has stirred up a lot of trouble for the leaders in Jerusalem. He just seemed to appear out of nowhere, dressed in camel's hair, living in the wild areas in the Jordan Valley. it is said he eats only what he can find in the wild—locusts, honey, other stuff. He has also stirred up a lot of hope—now there is a dangerous word. Hope always gets people in trouble, as if the Romans were not enough of a problem—now we might have hope of a better world, a new Israel. Fat chance with those crooks in the Temple! Anyway, I have decided to go with Yeshua so I can keep an eye on him and maybe keep him from doing something foolish, or unorthodox, or troublesome. If only he weren't so outspoken.

We set off early in the morning, making our way down the Jordan Valley, along the well-traveled trade route. We asked a caravan heading toward Galilee if they had heard about John the preacher and baptizer. They said he was further south, nearer to Jericho. We continued southward until almost sunset. Yeshua was a strong walker. He pointed to the west and said, "Beyond that ridge is Samaria. I want to visit there some day." He looked to the East, over the river, and said, "And we are close to the Jabbok where Jacob wrestled with Adonai." He paused a moment and then said, "I will come back here to spend some time in prayer." I looked toward the setting sun and said, "Why would you want to visit Samaria? You know they are our sworn enemies." He smiled and replied, "That is precisely why I want to visit them." He started to walk before I could say anything, before I could protest or warn him of the danger. He is truly a puzzle, this rabbi Yeshua.

We spent the night just off the road with another group of travelers. They offered us a place around their fire, which was a welcome warmth. The next morning, we started again very early and before noon had come upon a small crowd on the riverbank. "This must be him," said Yeshua. "Look at all the people. Some in the water. And such a variety—rich and poor. Even some Pharisees." We stood at the back of the crowd and watched and listened. John was about waist deep in the river. He began to preach: "Why did you come here? You are all like a bunch of snakes slithering away from a coming fire—looking for a place to be safe from Adonai's wrath. You want repentance? Then bear fruit worthy of it! Just because you can claim Abraham as your ancestor means nothing. Adonai can raise up children of Abraham from these stones on the river bank. If you are not a tree with good fruit, you will be cut down and thrown into a fire—burned up."

One man shouted, "What should we do?" John said, "Share what you have with the poor. If you have two coats, give one to the neighbor who has none. If you have some food, share it with the hungry. If you are a tax collector, take only what is due—no more." Suddenly there was a flurry of movement and the sound of metal. Someone called out, "Watch out!" as three Roman soldiers came through the crowd carrying long spears. I thought they had come to arrest John, but one of them said, "What about us?" John looked at them sternly and said, "Be fair! Don't threaten or abuse anyone! Don't extort money! Be satisfied with your pay!" Two of them went forward into the water and asked to be baptized; the third one stayed on the shore, looking nervously around. After the soldiers left, John continued, "I baptize you with water. But there is one coming whose sandal I am not worthy to untie. This one will baptize you with the Holy Spirit." He paused and then shouted, "And with fire!"

The crowd parted slightly as several well-dressed men from the Temple strutted forward. One of them called out, "Who do think you are? Are you a prophet? Or a messenger?" Then he laughed, "Or maybe even the Messiah?" John took a step closer to them and said, "I am the voice of one crying out: 'In the wilderness prepare the way of the Lord, make the paths straight.'" Several in the crowd yelled at the men from the Temple, "Go home! Go back to Jerusalem!" Then many people came forward to be baptized by John in the river. Rabbi Yeshua joined the line of people. I stayed on the bank.

John the Baptizer

EVEN INSIDE THIS PRISON cell, I can hear the music and dancing. I wonder who are Herod's guests tonight. I can smell the cooked meat despite the odor of piss and sweat in my cell. Herod is probably drunk already. But not Herodias. She is too afraid of losing control. I am sure this is all her doing after I told Herod he could not marry her. First, they were both already married. And then you cannot marry your brother's wife. Of course, he did anyway. I had to speak out in public against them both. Although that is not the worst thing either of them has done. Herod was afraid to arrest me because of what the people said about me being a prophet. He was afraid that I would start a rebellion. But Herodias had no such qualms, and she and her courtiers hated me and tried to spread rumors about me. So, I am not surprised that she convinced Antipas to have me arrested and put in prison. I am also not surprised that they put me so far away from Jerusalem. Machaereus is across the Dead Sea, in the desert of Moab, near the Nabateans. Some of my followers must have bribed a soldier because they showed up here asking to see me.

I wonder about that young rabbi, Yeshua Ben Joseph—the one from Nazareth, or was it Capernaum. He had come to be baptized, along with the rest of a long line of people. It is true I am given to having visions. And they come at the most unpredictable times. When I first saw him, I also thought I saw a bright light behind him. Then when he knelt in the water in front of me, I was sure I heard a voice—others later said that it was thunder. The voice was unclear, but it caused me to hesitate, and think maybe he should be baptizing me. He looked up at me and smiled, and said, "Don't be afraid." I poured water on his head and blessed him. As he turned and went back to the river bank, I was sure that I saw a dove fly down from the sky and land on his head or shoulder. What did this mean? Surely, he is destined for something important. When my followers came to visit me in prison,

I asked them to find this Yeshua and ask him, "Are you the one who is to come with fire? The one that God is sending to us? Or should we look for another?" I have not heard from them and probably never will.

The music has stopped. Probably the entertainment has finished. Herod has a reputation for inviting very young women to his parties. Since this one is for his birthday, some girls will probably be forced to dance for him. Who knows what else he will ask them to do for him before the night is over. If his guests have not already fallen asleep, drunk, they are probably making their way to their rooms. The guards are laughing, now cursing. Something unexpected must have happened. I'll try to get some sleep, too.

Jabal the Nabatean

I SAW HIM WHEN they brought him in a few days ago. He was really badly beaten. He had a certain pride about him—not high and mighty or arrogant—but more like confidence. He was very dark from the sun and unshaven. All he was wearing was a camel's hair tunic and leather sandals—both very worn. They locked him in a cell deep under the palace. His name was John.

I doubt I will see him again unless I am told to bring him some food. My family lives nearby. My father and uncle and some cousins work here at the fortress doing different jobs. My job here at Machaereus is to purchase food and other supplies—lots of wine—from the local markets. Some things the king brings with him from Jerusalem, or they buy in Jericho on the way. The nearest market is in Callirhoe by the Dead Sea. Sometimes I have to go all the way to Madaba, although when people hear Herod is coming to his fortress, they will often bring things to sell at the gate. Fruits and vegetables are quite easy to obtain. Meat and fresh fish are more difficult to find.

One of the guards told me that John was a traitor. He insulted the king and his new wife. Then he made an obscene gesture—they all hate the new queen and are not too fond of the king either. Some say he is not really a king, only a Roman puppet—then they dance around and fall down—then laugh. They may not like them, but they are still afraid of them. Anyone with the name of "Herod" is to be feared. The stories of this families' violence and treachery are legendary in Israel and in Nabataea. One guard told me he feels sorry for John, who he says is a holy prophet sent from God. He was baptized by John in the Jordan river a few months ago and has tried to live a better life since then.

It turns out I was right when I said that I would not see John again—he is dead. Last night was the king's birthday party and there were a lot of guests, so we had extra work to get things ready. The cooks were especially nervous and worried about pleasing the queen. It seems that the queen's daughter, Salome, was asked to dance for Herod. She must have put on quite a performance, because he stood up and promised to give her whatever she asked. The story goes that she ran to her mother, who whispered something in her ear. Then she went to Herod and asked for the head of John the baptizer on a plate. There was a hush in the room, and then some people laughed. Herod was clearly shocked, but since he had made an oath in public, he must not have wanted to appear weak. He called his guards and ordered them to do what Salome asked. Then he joked and ordered more wine for everyone. It must have been a grisly sight when they came back with John's bloody head on a platter. I was told that the young girl ran from the hall and wouldn't come back in.

A few days later, some of John's disciples came to the fortress and begged for his body. I spoke with one of them at the gate and offered some oranges for their journey. They thanked me and then said the strangest thing: "John told us to be prepared for the coming of the Messiah. Now we know he is here." I was about to ask them, "What is a Messiah?" but a soldier called to them, "He's over here on the garbage heap. Come and get what's left of him before the vultures do." I never got to ask my question. And I never saw them again.

Binyamin of Capernaum

AFTER THE BAPTISM, WE began our journey home to Galilee. Yeshua said he wanted to stop near the wadi Jabbok. He wanted to spend some time in prayer and reflection. "Who knows," he joked, "Maybe I will even get to wrestle with Adonai—like Jacob." I forced a smile and followed him on the path. It was a hot and dry day, so neither one of us talked much. After a few hours we were running low on water, so I took the gourds and went to find some. Yeshua sat down in the shade of a large rock. Another traveler pointed me toward a spring that was up the western slope of the valley. He said to look for a cluster of big stones and a few trees. I set off and after an hour or so found the spring. There were four or five people in front of me, so I sat down to wait my turn. I really needed a rest, anyway. I filled the gourds with water and began my descent down the valley. When I came back to the spot where I left Yeshua, he was nowhere in sight. I was not surprised—angry, but not surprised. It was very deserted and already getting dark. I called out, but there was no answer. I sat down and drank some water. When he did not come back soon, I opened my pouch and ate some bread and dried fish. I grumbled to myself and soon fell asleep.

I heard my name being called softly and my shoulder being shaken. It was morning and Yeshua was sitting beside me. "Where did you go?" I asked, trying not to sound too grumpy. He smiled and looked across the Jordan and said, "I went over to the wadi Jabbok." He pointed east, "Over there." "How did you get across the river?" I asked. He laughed and said, "Oh, I pretended I was Moses or Elijah and I just parted the waters of the river and walked across." I rolled over and grunted, "Very funny." He then said, "Well, you wouldn't believe me if I told you I walked across on top of the water, would you?" "That I would really like to see," I said with disdain. "Actually, I found a boatman who rowed me across." He paused and then, "He was there again this morning to bring me back." Yeshua looked back across the river. "Oh no," I thought. "He's got that 'far-away look' again." I sat up and said, "What happened—over there?" He said, "Do you believe in visions? Or dreams?" I said, "Well, sure—I guess so. Doesn't everybody? Did you wrestle with Adonai?"

Yeshua then said, "No. I think it was 'The Tempter'—Satan—Beelzebul. It was dark—I was praying. Then I heard a voice—I think. 'Are you hungry?' I looked up, but there was no one there. Then again, 'Are you hungry?' I said, 'Yes. I'm hungry.' Then the voice said the strangest thing: 'Since you are the Son of the Most High, change these stones into bread.' I looked around and there were a lot of stones. I was even tempted to try it—why not! Then I thought maybe this was a test, so I said, 'We do not live by bread alone, but by all the words of Adonai.' There was silence—for what seemed like a long time. Then the voice said, 'Stand up! Come with me!' So, I stood and then I seemed to be flying. I closed my eyes. And when I opened them, I was on the roof of the Temple—the highest spot. I got dizzy, then the voice said to me again: 'Since you are the Son of the Most High, throw yourself down, for it is written 'The angels of heaven will protect you—they will bear you up so that you do not smash your foot against a stone.'" I looked at Yeshua in disbelief. "I know," he said. "It sounds strange—but it was all so real." "What did you do?" I asked. "Well, I looked away, and then said: 'It is also written, "Do not put Adonai to the test." And right away I was back at the wadi Jabbok—alone—dazed; but alone."

I was wide awake by then. Yeshua continued looking across the river. "Was that the end?" I asked. He was quiet for a moment and then said, "No. There was one more test. I waited for a time and finally the voice came again. 'Stand up! Come with me!' and I was in a whirlwind. This time I was at the top of a mountain, maybe Carmel or maybe Mount Hermon—I don't know. I could see as far as Damascus and Babylon and Alexandria and lots of other great cities. It was all very glorious. Then the voice said to me, 'All that you see before you I can give to you. All you have to do is bow down and worship me. It can all be yours.'" "What did you say?" I asked. Yeshua looked very serious and then laughed. "I told the Tempter to go away and bother someone else. For it is written: 'You shall worship only Adonai and serve only that one.' Suddenly everything vanished and I was back at wadi Jabbok—in the dark. I was exhausted. And I was still hungry."

I looked at him and said, "That was some vision. Were you afraid? I mean, afraid of the Tempter? I know I would have been." He looked at the ground and said softly, "Being near the Tempter was not the most frightening thing. It was what he said to me." He paused and shuddered, "That I am the Son of the Most High—that was the most frightening thing anyone could say to me." I did not know what to say, so I said nothing. Finally, Yeshua said, "I am famished. Is there any bread or fish left?" I silently handed him the sack with what was left. One more thing I still wonder about: how did he get across the Jordan River? I sure don't buy that cockamamie story about there being a boatman handy at the shore. Maybe he is more like Moses and Elijah than I thought.

Simon of Capernaum

WE HAD BEEN OUT on the lake all night and had caught nothing. Andrew was dozing off. James and John and their father Zebedee were not far off in the other boat. They had caught nothing, too. As usual, James and John were arguing about whose fault it was that we had caught not one fish. The sun was just rising in the east. There was a slight fog over the water. Everything was gray and quiet. I looked down the shoreline and saw two figures walking toward us. I soon recognized them as that new rabbi, Yeshua, and his shadow—Binyamin—what a pest. They stopped and looked out at us. Rabbi Yeshua was calling out to us, but I could not hear what he was saying. I called to John, "What is he saying?" John shouted back, "He wants to know if we have caught any fish." I shrugged, then shouted to him, "No! We have tried all night—but nothing—empty nets!" He called back, "Throw your nets over the right side of the boat. I think you will have better luck." James laughed and yelled, "So now he is not only the rabbi, but the big fisherman, too. Who does he think he is? I'll bet he hasn't pulled a net a day in his life. 'Try the right side of the boat!'—what a joke." Peter called back, "Don't be so sure. I've seen him do some strange and amazing things. I think we should try it. What do we have to lose?"

Well, we dropped the nets over the right side of each boat—James and John grumbling the whole time. I pulled in the sail to give us some forward movement. Suddenly the boat shuddered and stopped. The ropes on the nets tightened. Andrew and I jumped to the side and pulled. I looked over and James and John were doing the same thing. "We've got something!" called Zebedee. We all pulled and pulled and soon hauled in a huge catch. "There's too many," cried Andrew. "What will we do with all these fish?" "Sell 'em and eat 'em!" I yelled as I pulled in the net. After we hauled in the catch, we made for the shore. Rabbi Yeshua and Binyamin were waiting for us—both grinning from ear to ear. They had started a fire. "Bring some fish," the rabbi called. "I may not know how to catch them, but at least I know how to grill them." I grabbed two good-sized fish and quickly gutted them and washed them in the lake. I brought them to the fire, and the rabbi stuck a long sharp stick down the mouth of each and held them over the fire. I said nothing.

When the fish were ready and we had all eaten some, rabbi Yeshua and I walked down to the lake to wash our hands. I spoke to him in a quiet voice: "You probably know I am not a perfect Jew. I have a bad temper and I have been known to get into a few fights. I don't always show up at the synagogue. I even swear more than I should. What I am trying to say is that I am a sinful man. I don't deserve what you did for us today." I paused and dried my hands on my shirt. I remember he said, "But you are a good fisherman." I nodded, "Well, yes I am—Andrew, too. And James and John" He looked out over the lake for a few moments, then turned to me with his dark eyes, and said, "Stick with me and I will make you fish for people." I didn't know what he meant by that. But I knew he had a plan. And, for whatever hair-brained reason, I felt I wanted—no, needed—to be a part of it.

Ruth of Nazareth

I WISH I COULD stop crying, but I can't. This has been a horrible day. I don't know if I am frightened or angry or disappointed or maybe all of them together. A few days ago, I was excited and happy—Yeshua was coming back to Nazareth to preach in our synagogue. I had talked with Mary at the well, and she had told me he was coming on the next day. Then she said that I might wear my bright blue shawl to attract his attention. She looked at me with a smile and I knew she knew how much I loved him. I said nothing, just nodded my head. I wished Yeshua could see me becoming a strong woman, as I lifted my water jug to my shoulder—and a good cook—and weaver. I remember how dizzy I felt as I walked home. I couldn't contain my excitement, so I told my Aunt Leah. I knew she would not gossip to anyone. She laughed and teased me, "Oh! Young love is sooooo obvious. Everyone will know by the way you look at him. And he is very handsome. But he is sooooo serious!" I must have blushed bright red because I felt so hot.

What a fool I was. Everything went wrong. I made up some lame excuse to stop and visit Mary. I acted surprised to see him. He was very polite, and told me how much I had grown, and that some young man will be lucky to have me for his wife. I thanked him and then asked him about Capernaum. He told me he was adjusting and was even becoming quite good at fishing. He told me about receiving the old rabbi's house and library. He was thrilled that he now had so many scrolls to study. I wished he would stop smiling and looking at me. Then he said that he had come to Nazareth to convince his mother to come to Capernaum to live with him. He looked away, and then said that he had decided not to marry, and needed someone to care for his house. I almost said I would help, but bit my lip instead. I wanted to ask him why he had decided not to marry, but that would have been too obvious—too forward. Now I wish I had asked him—and screamed at him—and pushed him into a corner. But I turned and ran out the door so he would not see my tears.

The next day was the worst. It was Shabbat, and we were gathering at the synagogue. Instead of my bright blue shawl, I wore my black one. My Aunt Leah frowned at me when we sat down in the back. Our rabbi began with a long prayer. Then we said some psalms. When it was time for the sermon, he introduced Yeshua and praised his family and how much we missed his father, Joseph, and were so blessed by his mother and sisters and brothers. Then he praised Rabbi Ben Sirach for teaching Yeshua and for choosing him to be the next rabbi of Capernaum. I silently wished Yeshua had never met that old man. Finally, he asked Yeshua to come forward and give the sermon. He rose and stepped to the front and then asked for the scroll of the prophet Isaiah. He unrolled it and found the place and began to read:

"The Spirit of Adonai is upon me, because Adonai has anointed me to bring good news to the poor. Adonai has sent me to proclaim release to the captives, and recovery of sight to the blind, to let the oppressed go free, to proclaim the year of Adonai's jubilee."

Then he sat down and said, "Today this prophecy has been fulfilled in your hearing." All the elders nodded in agreement and some looked around at Mary and said how proud she must be. Others patted his brothers on their backs. Then he began again: "Repent and prepare for the coming of the kingdom of heaven. Do not think of yourselves as special, as above others." Someone spoke up: "Are you saying we are not worthy?" I was getting nervous. Yeshua said, "No doubt you have heard that I have healed some in Capernaum, and now you want me to do the same here. But in order for me to do that you must have faith." Someone else said, "So now we are not only unworthy, but we have no faith!" The synagogue was becoming restless, and I was becoming worried. Yeshua continued: "Adonai has a special place for the outcast and the poor, the ones we too often think of as outside our mercy and love. Remember, in the days of Elijah, when there was a drought for over three years, and there was severe famine? And there were many widows in our land, yet Elijah was sent to none of them. But he was sent to the widow in Zarephath, in Sidon, of all places. And in the days of Elisha, there were many lepers in our land. But none of them were cleansed but Naaman the Syrian. Yes, we are chosen—but we are chosen to give mercy, not judgment—to promote forgiveness, not purity." There was a stunned silence. Then murmurs, then voices got louder. One elder stood up and said: "We hear that you have healed many in Capernaum. Do the same here in Nazareth! Or are we not good enough!" Yeshua replied: "Truly, truly, I tell you, no prophet is accepted in the prophet's home town."

I couldn't believe what I was hearing. Part of me was dumbstruck by the power of his words. Another part of me was petrified since many of the men were now shouting at him: "Who do you think you are?" "You should be stoned!" "Let's throw him out!" "Over the cliff!" Some men grabbed Yeshua and pushed him into the street. I saw Hassan and said, "Do something! Help him!" Hassan found Yaakov and Judah, two of Yeshua's brothers, but it was too late. The mob had driven him out of town toward the cliffs, shouting all the way. I just sat down and stared at the ground. Aunt Leah came over and put her arms around me. After some time, Hassan came back. "What happened?" I asked. "Nothing," he said. "They pushed him toward the cliff, and then Yeshua just turned around and looked at them all, and walked away, back into town, into his house. Everyone went home." I left the synagogue and hesitated at their house. I knocked on their door and Mary came and said they would both be leaving tomorrow to go to Capernaum. Young Joseph would keep the house since he has a growing family. I thanked her and said a blessing. I then realized that Yeshua was not only walking out of Nazareth, but out of my life, too—probably forever.

Mary

AM I A BAD mother? When did I become such a terrible mother? In the end, I had to do everything with my own hands. Miracles don't happen when your existence is tied to an oven or a house or a garden. I had waited for a miracle. A miracle for me and my first-born son. It never came. There were lots of other miracles for lots of other people—but not for me. I had the other children to think of. I had the family reputation to worry about. I should have insisted that he marry Ruth. We all knew that she was in love with him. I never should have let him go to Capernaum. I blame that old rabbi. I blame Simon and his friends. I blame all those others who call themselves disciples—followers. And most of all, I blame Adonai. I never should have listened to that voice. I should have plugged my ears and imagined it all as a bad dream. We might still be in Bethlehem. Yeshua might have remained a carpenter like his father—like his father—his far-away father, now so far away, who is powerless to help, to save, to rescue from even his own neighbors. No wonder people say, "Can anything good come out of Nazareth!"

I have decided to move to Capernaum. Who else will watch over him? Who else will do his wash, cook his meals, mend his tunics? I will miss the children and the grandchildren. It is not so far from Nazareth, but it will be lonely, I think. I will have to get used to cleaning and cooking fish—not my favorite. I am sure I can plant a garden. And there will be other widows— like Simon's mother. And the lake is beautiful, even in a storm. But I fear for him. He has already angered people here in Nazareth. There were two visitors from Jerusalem on that Sabbath. I am sure they will tell the other Pharisees and scribes in Jerusalem. And what about Herod? And what about the Romans? They hate any disruptions. And they kill people with little reason. When Joseph and I dedicated Yeshua in the Temple, when he was circumcised, an old man blessed us with a psalm, but then whispered to me that a sword would one day pierce my heart. I fear it will come sooner than I can prepare for it.

I have already packed some of my things. I will leave most of it here for Joseph, who already has a wife and two children. Simon and Miriam have a little girl, and Elizabeth is expecting in a few months. They will all need things that we had collected over the years. Yaakov, the eldest, and Judah, the youngest, will help carry things to Capernaum. Neither of them is married yet, so they can be away for a few days. Maybe one of them will stay in Capernaum. Who knows? I thought that my days of being unsettled were over long ago. I think I am just beginning a new time of change and restlessness. Surely that is the best word to describe Yeshua—restless. I think I am too old for all of this.

Andrew of Capernaum

SIMON'S WIFE THINKS WE have lost our minds. So does my cousin Miriam. "Why would you give up a thriving fishing trade to follow some crazy rabbi with a plan to change the world?" she said. I told her he does not want to change the entire world, just reform and renew Israel—to make us more loving and kinder. He keeps quoting the prophets who said that Adonai wants mercy not sacrifices, justice not condemnation. He talks a lot about the least, the lost, and the little ones. "And how about the Romans?", she asked. "Is he going to change and reform them, too?" I told her that the Romans are also our neighbors and we should treat them as such. I remember that did not go over so well the first time he preached it, but I know it caused people to think. She laughed and said, "You would do better joining the Zealots. At least they know how to deal with the Romans." And then she added with a sneer, "You are just doing this because Simon agreed to it." I jumped up and told her, "No! I was the first to agree. I said 'Yes!' right away. Simon said he wanted to think about it." I hated when people saw me as the little brother. My whole life everyone said, "Oh, you must be Simon's little brother." Well, this time I was the first to respond when Yeshua asked us to follow him on his journey, his mission. I know it was impulsive, but I was tired of being 'Simon's little brother.'

I remember that day. It was late in the afternoon, and we were still washing and mending our nets along the shoreline. Yeshua was helping us, and we were talking about the good weather and the chances of a storm. James and John were close by, arguing as usual. Their father, Zebedee, was still in the boat with their hired hands. I think they were patching a leak in the bow. Yeshua said to us, "Tonight I want you to help me with the healings. There will be many people from the area who will come to the synagogue with their sick and possessed friends and relatives. They will want me to pray over them and lay hands on them. They will want me to heal them like I healed the man with the unclean spirit last week. I will try—but I will need help." We were all silent for a while. Then he said, "I want you to become my disciples and follow me on a mission to preach good news to my people, cast out demons, and silence the evil spirits." He paused and looked at each of us. Then he laughed and said, "Well, you are all fishermen, aren't you? Now you will be fishing for—people."

I stood up right away and said, "I'll do it! I will follow." I looked at Simon, and James, and John. They were all startled. Then John stood up and then James. They did not speak, just nodded their heads. We all looked at Simon, who continued to fiddle with the net. He then looked up and said he would have to think about it—talk to his wife. He looked at James and John and said, "What about Zebedee?" John said he still has the hired men and they would help out when they could. Yeshua said, "This will not be easy. I am asking you to give up a lot for the sake of the coming reign of Adonai. We will travel a lot—even up to Jerusalem to confront the priests and scribes. Do you remember the farmer outside of Capernaum who wanted to build a watchtower on his land? Remember how he started with great fanfare, but then ran out of money so could never complete the tower? People laughed at him because he did not plan well. We must plan well." He stood up and looked at us: "Will you come to the synagogue this evening after supper?" We all agreed. He smiled at us and turned to go home.

Evenings were usually quiet in Capernaum. But tonight was different. As we walked toward the synagogue, we were aware of the hum of voices and an unusually large number of people in the streets—some we knew, some were strangers. The square in the middle of town was full: there were old people on pallets, some blind and lame, and most troubling were those squirming and screaming, probably possessed. Andrew shook his head and said, "How are we going to do anything with this mob. I hope Rabbi Yeshua has a plan." I said nothing, but I knew he had something in mind. We made our way through the crowd. Someone yelled at us, "Hey! Wait your turn! We were here before you!" I nodded and said we were here to help the Rabbi. We pushed through and into the synagogue, only to find it just as crowded. Yeshua was sitting and holding a young man who looked like he was asleep. A woman was crying and kept repeating, "My son—he hasn't slept in days—and now he is so peaceful. I can't believe it." Simon went over and picked up the young man and carried him outside, followed by his mother. Yeshua called us over and said. "Try to keep the people in line. It is going to be a long night. James and John, keep an eye out for those who are possessed and might become violent. Be as gentle as you can and bring them to me." Then he motioned to me and said, "Andrew, sit here and lay your hands on those who have a fever or sickness. Pray to Adonai for healing power." And so, we passed the next few hours healing and praying. When a possessed person came to us, Yeshua commanded the demon to be silent and come out. I was more frightened than when I was in a storm on the Gennesaret, but I kept praying and blessing. By midnight all had gone and I was exhausted. James, John, and Simon sat down as if in shock. John said to his brother, "What just happened?" James said, "I don't know. I feel like Jacob at Jabbok—'Surely Adonai was in this place and I did not know it.'" Yeshua looked at us and said, "Go home and get some sleep. There will be more to do tomorrow." I went home, but I could not sleep.

James of Capernaum

MOST OF OUR LIVES had been routine. Day after day, the same thing. We had worn a path between home and the fishing boats—home and the fishing boats. We would go to synagogue on Shabbat, to my wife's parents' once a week, to Simon's to talk about boat and net repairs, to John's to complain about Simon. There was an occasional wedding feast or festival, but it was mostly same old routine week after week, year after year. We had talked about moving south to become farmers, or buying some olive groves, but all we had ever known was fishing. John had even joked about joining the Zealots and fighting the Romans—at least I think he was joking.

Then one day our rabbi told us he was too old and tired to continue. He had asked a young man from Nazareth, one Yeshua ben Joseph, to come and be our rabbi. We had seen him at Rabbi Ben-Sirach's home, and he had spoken at our synagogue a few times, so we were not surprised. There were some complaints: he is too young, not yet forty years old; he is not from Capernaum; he is not married. But we trusted Rabbi Ben-Sirach, so life went on, and our new rabbi arrived with his mother. We expected things to return to normal—we were very wrong. One day he produced a huge catch of fish after a night of nothing, then he cured a lame child, cast out a demon, and turned quiet Capernaum on its head. Most importantly, at least for me—and John, Andrew, and Simon—he called us to follow him on an adventure—to preach good news, to heal the sick, to teach about Adonai's mercy and love for all people. We were all excited but scared at the same time. We knew we would be going against traditions and we would find resistance, even violence.

We began to go out from Capernaum into the countryside of Galilee and were well received. People were generous, fed us, and gave us places to rest. But not everyone was welcoming and glad to see us. The Pharisees were particularly critical and spoke against us. Yeshua had told us we would need some more disciples to help with the mission, so it did not surprise us when he called several more Galileans: Philip, Bartholomew, Thaddeus, and James ben Alphaeus. Having two disciples named James was confusing, so Yeshua gave me and John the nickname of "Boanerges"—sons of thunder. I have never been sure if that was a compliment or not. We were quite surprised when he called Thomas because he asked so many questions. It really surprised us when he called Simon, a Canaanite—a real outsider. But the most surprising choice was Levi, who was a tax collector. The only Israelites who did not hate, and fear, tax collectors were the rich ones who were collaborating with the Romans. Most of them were in Jerusalem, and—sorry to say—many were in the Temple. The Romans were smart enough to hire local Jews to do their dirty work of collecting taxes for everything they could get. The tax collectors, in order to make their own money, had to extort extra money from the farmers and fishermen and townspeople. The Romans did not care how they did it as long as they were paid their taxes on time. So, for Yeshua to choose a tax collector was a very radical move. It is not surprising that Levi had a second name: he was also known as Matthew. Having him as a fellow disciple was not easy. It took a long time for us to learn to trust him.

Shortly after Yeshua called Levi to be a disciple, he invited us to his home for a dinner with friends. There were quite a few other tax collectors and some folks who would not be welcome in many homes in Israel. Yeshua had made it clear that we are to be open to all—"Sinners welcome!" he would often say to us. We were eating on an open terrace when some Pharisees came by and called out to us: "Why is your rabbi eating with tax collectors and sinners?" Before we could answer, Yeshua stood up and said to them: "Those who are healthy have no need of a physician, but those who are sick. I have come not for the righteous," then he paused and glared at them, "but for sinners." Then he sat down and asked for some more wine. I had a hard time containing my laughter, even though I knew I should not gloat when those pious Pharisees get put in their place. Humility is still a challenge for me. I looked over at my brother John, who was also laughing. He called out, "Maybe they would like to join us?" I laughed again, but I did not like the look the Pharisees gave us as they walked away, whispering to themselves. I called to John, "They are probably plotting a way to get rid of us." Then I laughed some more. It was a great night.

Jannai the Lame

YESTERDAY I WAS OUT walking—again. I still have to use a cane, and it helps to have one of the neighbor's children to lean on now and then. As I came into the village square, Jonas shook his fist and called out, "You still owe me for those repairs to my roof." Then he laughed loudly and slapped his friend on the shoulder: "He still thinks I am going to charge him. For what? A miracle! How can you pay for a miracle?" Then he looked at me kindly and said, "Have a nice walk. Not too far, now!"

Until recently, I thought I would never walk again. When I was a child, I had an illness that left me lame—unable to walk. I was confined to my bed, or a chair. I lived with my parents and one sister. I had learned to weave baskets for a living, but I could not join in much of the village life. I never went fishing. I never climbed an olive tree. I rarely got to the synagogue. I had to give up my dream of one day going to Jerusalem for Passover. But now—maybe next year! Rabbi Ben-Sirach came to visit me at least once a week, but it was not the same as being with the entire congregation. When he died, I was very depressed. I still miss him a lot. He made me laugh—and cry—sometimes at the same time. I heard the news that the village was getting a new rabbi, a young man from Nazareth. I never got to meet him until that fateful day.

My sister came home one evening full of excitement and told us that the new rabbi was a miracle worker—a healer. "He could cast out demons! He cured Elihu's son of his fits and outbursts. He healed Joanna's daughter of whatever was wrong with her—she can smile now—she can smile." We were all amazed and maybe a little frightened by this strange new authority in our young rabbi. The next day I was busy weaving a basket when four of my neighbors came bursting through the door. They told me that Rabbi Yeshua was at Jonas' house and a crowd was gathering asking for healings and blessings. They told me to lie down on my pallet and put away my basket. They were going to take me to be healed. I really did not have a choice, so I lay down and held on as they carried me out the door and down the street. When we arrived at Jonas' house, there was a vast crowd around the door so we could not get through. Barnabas tried to push his way through but could not budge the crowd. Then he said, "The roof—let's take him to the roof!" They carried me around to the side of the house and up the stairs that led to the roof. It was the first time that I realized I was afraid of heights. Then they tore off the plaster and tiles. I told them to stop, but they did not listen. Barnabas said they would lower me down so I could be healed. He ran down the steps to find some rope. By this time the people in the house were looking up to see who was tearing off the roof. Jonas was shouting angrily at us, but he could do nothing because of the crowd. When Barnabas came back, they attached ropes to my pallet and slowly lowered me down through the roof. I have to admit I was very frightened.

Rabbi Yeshua looked up at my friends and laughingly said to the crowd, "Here are people of great faith. Even a roof won't stop them from helping their neighbor." Then he looked at me with great kindness. He touched my legs and then my head and said, "My son, your sins are forgiven." Not what I expected. There were some religious scribes in the crowd who immediately stood up and said, "Who do you think you are? This is blasphemy! Only Adonai can forgive sins!" Yeshua turned to them and said, "I sense that you have questions in your hearts about healing and forgiveness. Now, which is easier to say to this lame man, 'Your sins are forgiven,' or to say 'Stand up! Pick up your pallet and go home'?" He paused a moment, but they gave no reply. Then he stood up and said, "So that you all may know that the Son of Man has authority here to forgive sins"—then he looked down at me and said, "I say to you, Stand up! Take up your pallet! And go to your home!" I was both shocked and afraid. I felt a strange new power, so I lifted my legs, slowly pushed myself up, and tried to stand up. I was weak—wobbly—but I was standing. I couldn't believe it. I almost lost my balance, and then a cheer went up from the crowd. I reached down and lifted my pallet and walked out the door—tears streaming down my face. Someone in the crowd whispered, "We have seen nothing like this before." I agreed—I agreed.

Barnabas and his friends wanted to help me carry my pallet, but I told them, "No! I want to do this on my own." I took a few steps and then turned back and said, "Tomorrow I will help you fix Jonas' roof." They all laughed as I slowly made my way home, singing, "Praise the Lord, O my soul."

Aaron of Tiberias: A Scribe

WORD HAD SPREAD QUICKLY about the young rabbi at Capernaum. We had heard of him through Rabbi Ben-Sirach at our regular gathering of rabbis and scribes and other Pharisees. He told us how intelligent and imaginative he was. He was amazed at how quickly he understood Torah and tradition. After his first sermon in Capernaum, we asked him what he talked about. Ben-Sirach smiled and said, "He spoke of mercy and forgiveness. He also said we needed to be prepared for some new things Adonai had in store for us. I think he was quoting from Isaiah—I think he really likes Isaiah above all the other prophets: 'Watch out,' he said, 'I am doing a new thing. Don't you see it? Even now it springs forth!'" Then he turned to us and said, "I think you will like him. You will not always agree with him—but then who in this crowd ever agrees with anyone else—so he will fit in." We were all puzzled by what he meant by 'fit in.' Then he told us he was going to invite Yeshua ben Joseph of Nazareth to be the rabbi in Capernaum when he retired. Eliezar immediately said, "But he is so young. And we have not examined him. We do not know if he is, well, strict enough to be a rabbi." Many of the others agreed. Then Ben-Sirach quietly grumbled, "Even Elijah would not be pure enough for some of you." I had to laugh, but quietly, since this group has little sense of humor. We moved on to other things, but I made it a point to meet this Yeshua.

Not long after that gathering, Rabbi Ben-Sirach took ill and died. We all were present at this funeral, but I did not have a chance to talk with the young rabbi. He led the funeral service with great respect and humility. He already seemed to be very popular with the people, especially a group of fishermen and their families. A few weeks later, I learned Yeshua had moved to Capernaum with his mother and become the rabbi there. Soon I was hearing some strange things about his ministry. It was rumored that he had healed several local people and cast out some evil spirits. Word about him was spreading. Three of us from Tiberias decided to go up to Capernaum and meet him. When we got to the village, there was a huge crowd around one of the homes. We were told that Rabbi Yeshua was inside teaching and healing. We asked to enter and were respectfully invited to come in.

By the time we found a place to sit down, there were already two people who had been healed and were weeping at his feet. Suddenly we noticed some falling plaster and looked up at the ceiling where some men on the roof had ripped open a large hole. A large man, presumably the owner of the house, began yelling at them to stop, but to no avail. We all moved to avoid being hit with chunks of tile from the roof. When the hole was large enough, they lowered a man on a pallet down into the center of the room. One man on the roof hollered, "He can't walk! He is lame! We want you to help him!" Rabbi Yeshua smiled up at them and said they must have great faith to tear off a roof for a friend. He looked at the lame man and reached out and touched his legs. Then he reached into a pouch and took out some oil, poured some on the man's legs and massaged them. Then he put his hands on the lame man's head and said, "My son, your sins are forgiven." My colleague Eliezar was on his feet immediately and shouted: "That is blasphemy! Only Adonai can forgive sins! Who do you think you are?"

Rabbi Yeshua calmly looked at Eliezar and said, "Why do you question in your hearts my authority to forgive sins?" When no one answered, he asked, "Which is easier to say, 'Your sins are forgiven,' or to say, 'Stand up! Pick up your pallet and go home?'" Eliezar said nothing—only glared. Then Rabbi Yeshua stood up with equal anger and said, "So that you all will know that the Son of Man has the power to forgive sins," then he pointed to the lame man, "I say to you, 'Stand up! Pick up your pallet and go home!'" Everyone was silent. Then the lame man sat up, placed his feet on the ground and struggled to get up. His legs collapsed at first, but then he was standing, unsteady at first, but standing. There were gasps from the crowd, then a few cries, and then a cheer. The lame man bent down and picked up his pallet and walked out the door. One man on the roof called down, "Don't worry, Jonas. We will fix your roof."

The three of us did not know what to do, so we left. Eliezar was so mad he just kept walking. Levi and I found some shade and sat down. After a while he said to me, "What do you think? What do you make of all that?" I took a sip of water from a jug and then said, "Well, we cannot deny that he has the power of healing. That was very impressive—remarkable by any standard." I paused a moment and then continued: "Actually, I am more concerned about his reference to the Son of Man. Was he actually implying that he was the Son of Man, or was he referring to someone else?" Levi just shook his head and said, "I don't know. Maybe—maybe not. Whoever he thinks he is, he clearly believes that he has the power to forgive sins. And that is a problem—a big problem."

I agreed that claiming the power to forgive sins was an issue, but I was equally concerned about the reference to the Son of Man. This figure is closely linked to prophecies of the Day of Adonai, when the whole world will be changed, and the Kingdom of Israel will be re-established; there will be great destruction, justice will be meted out, and the righteous will rule. We rabbis do not talk much about it. We hear it from our brothers, the Essenes, as well as in the war cries of the young Zealots. Frankly, I get frustrated hearing people say that they see signs of the end of the world and Armageddon and the last judgment. They think every rumor or massacre or earthquake is a sign of something or other. If this young rabbi becomes identified with the Son of Man, we are in for a lot of trouble and he will not be able to control it. The Romans and the religious folks in Jerusalem won't like it either. I think Rabbi Yeshua needs to slow down and be careful not to upset the people in power. But from what I witnessed today, I think that is unlikely.

Hannah of Capernaum

I WAS ALONE AGAIN. The crowd had all gone off with Rabbi Yeshua to the home of Jairus, the synagogue leader. I was used to being alone, but now there was hope. Soon I might be able to rejoin the community and my family. I felt badly that I had kept the Rabbi from going directly to the home of Jairus, whose daughter had been so sick and maybe even near death. But I was desperate. My condition had gone on for twelve years. I had spent all my money on doctors and healers, and nothing seemed to work. I could not stop the bleeding. I was ready to give up and die. Praise the Lord I didn't.

It all began many years ago. I was young and healthy. I was surrounded by a loving family with many friends, and my marriage had been arranged for several years. I had known my future husband since I was a child and was happy with our future together. I had been married for less than a year when I became pregnant. My husband and I hoped for a son. We would name him Samuel. My husband's business was prospering; my friends and neighbors were glad for us; my family was overjoyed. After a few months, I felt weak and fainted several times. My mother made me stay in bed most of the day and brought me fresh goat's milk to give me strength. It was of no use. I began to bleed and then lost the baby. Everyone was kind and many of the women said, "Well, sometimes this happens, but don't worry. You can try again in a few months." After a few months, I was still bleeding. Of course, this meant I was 'unclean', so I could not sleep with my husband, or go to synagogue, or be present at family and community events. I thought this condition would end soon. I was wrong.

After five years, my husband asked for a divorce and I agreed. I felt he needed to have a family and a legacy, and I was in the way. He agreed to find me a place to live and continued to support me as best he could. A wealthy cousin from Sepphoris helped to pay for some doctors, but nothing seemed to help. I was isolated and alone. Fortunately, some villagers kept me busy with weaving and clothing repairs, so I survived. They would bring the clothing to a large basket outside my door and leave it—never handing it to me directly. When the repairs were finished, I would place them back in the basket, and they would collect it and leave some money. We never spoke or came close and—Adonai forbid—we never touched. I could walk into the village and was always careful to keep my distance from everyone. This was as painful as the bleeding itself.

One day I overheard some people talking about the new rabbi named Yeshua. He had come from Nazareth to replace Rabbi Ben Sirach. I had never met him, but word had spread that he was a wonderful preacher and also had the power to heal and cast out demons. He had gathered around him some of the young men of the town and had traveled to some other villages nearby. I saw one of my former neighbors and risked asking her about Rabbi Yeshua. "Is he here in Capernaum?" I asked. She hesitated, turned away, then quickly said, "He has gone across the lake with his disciples. He will be back tomorrow. He might help you if you ask him." She smiled at me and walked on. As I walked home, I felt depressed because I had been hopeful, so many times, for so many years, only to be disappointed again and again. I decided that tomorrow I would try one more time.

I woke early and finished some sewing. I left my house and walked toward the lake where I expected to find him. There was already a great crowd around him and he was teaching them. I stood at the back of the crowd, not daring to get too close to anyone. I was gathering my courage when Jairus, one leader of the synagogue, came rushing through the crowd, kneeling in front of Rabbi Yeshua. I could not hear what he was saying, so I asked a nearby woman. She told me that Jairus little daughter was gravely ill and near death and he asked the Rabbi to come and heal her. I was afraid I would now miss my chance. The crowd then turned to follow Rabbi Yeshua. As they passed by me, I said to myself, "If only I can touch the hem of his robe, I might be cured." I knelt down and as he walked past me, I reached out and grabbed the edge of his robe. I felt a shock and a burning feeling in my womb. Suddenly, I was aware that the Rabbi had stopped. He turned and said, "Who touched me?" Everyone looked startled. One of his disciples said, "What do you mean 'Who touched me?' Look at the crowd around you. It could have been anyone." Rabbi Yeshua said, "No! Someone touched me with a purpose. I felt power go out from me." I was petrified. I came forward, and the crowd kept their distance from me. I knelt down and told him I was the one who had grasped his robe. Before I knew it, my entire story had poured out. He must have thought I was a babbling fool. But instead, he knelt down and took my hands—imagine that. I wept as he said to me, "Daughter! Your faith has made you well. Go in peace and be healed of your illness."

As I was sitting by the lake all alone, some of the crowd came back talking wildly. "What happened?" I asked. They seemed to recognize that I was now a different person. They came close and told me how Jairus' daughter was believed to be dead and that Rabbi Yeshua told them she was only sleeping and then he raised her up and healed her. "From death," they said. "Can you imagine! He brought her to life again." I smiled and said, "Yes! I can imagine such a thing. In fact, I am sure of it."

Simon the Canaanite

I STILL GET "THE look" from some of the Galileans. You know, "the look" means that "we still aren't sure that we trust you," or "just remember you are one of us, but know your place." I have been used to it much of my life. I had hoped it would be different here with Rabbi Yeshua. I grew up in the coastal plain north of Mount Carmel, near ancient Acco. My people were called Canaanites, sometimes Phoenicians, but my family had long ago become Jews. My father was a leader in our synagogue—a follower of the Pharisees and very strict in following all the rules and especially the Sabbath observances. I was strict, too, but I was also looking for some excitement. Several of the young men in our community had run off to join the Zealots, to attack and harass the Romans who patrolled the highways and trade routes. Two of them have been killed. My father would growl and stomp around: "Who do they think they are? Judas Maccabeus? Or maybe King David?" I stood up for the Zealots, saying that they were defending the Torah and the purity of the land and the people. At least the Zealots were doing something instead of just sitting around. My father said, "I, too, will die for my beliefs. But I am not willing to kill for them. Besides, when Messiah comes, he will rid us of all evil and make Israel clean again." He paused a moment and then said, "They should stay at home and get married and work hard—AND study the Torah!" He always finished his tirades with "AND study the Torah!" I wasn't ready to get married, but I did work hard and study the Torah—a lot. But there was something missing.

I heard my parents talking one night about our cousins in Tyre who needed help to rebuild part of their house. So, I volunteered to go north to help for a few days. I was amazed when they said, "Yes. That would be a good thing to do." The next morning, I packed my clothes and a few tools and some food for the trip. I set out on the road north toward Tyre. The weather was decent and there was a cool breeze coming from the sea. As I neared the city, I noticed a group of twenty or thirty people off to the side of the road. I assumed they had stopped to eat, but then I noticed they were in a circle around a young man who was speaking to them. I decided to join the group and sat down at the edge of the group. This was as good a time as any to eat some bread and cheese, so I opened my sack and ate. Just then someone in the crowd asked the young man, "Rabbi, why do your disciples not follow the traditions of the elders and wash their hands before they eat?" I nearly choked on my bread because I suddenly realized that I, too, had not washed my hands before I ate—nor had I offered a blessing. So, he is a Rabbi, and so young. I suddenly became more interested in what he would say. The young Rabbi thought for a moment and then said, "Listen! It is not what goes into the mouth that defiles a person, but what comes out of the mouth." One man close to him said, "Do you know the Pharisees were offended when you said this same thing before?" I said to myself, "I know my father would be offended." Then the young man lowered his voice and said, "If a blind man leads another blind person, will they not both fall into the pit? The Pharisees are blind guides. Remember what Isaiah said: 'This people honor me with their lips but their hearts are far from me; in vain do they worship me, teaching human precepts as divine doctrines.'" I was stunned. I stopped eating. There was silence.

I think the young man felt he needed to explain himself so he continued: "Do you not see that whatever goes into the mouth enters the stomach and then goes out into the sewer? But what comes out of the mouth proceeds from the heart, and this is what defiles a person. For from out of the heart come evil intentions, murder, adultery, fornication, theft, false witness, slander—all contrary to Torah, and to love of God and neighbor. These are what defile a person, but to eat with unwashed hands does not defile." Some people nodded in agreement, but others turned away and grumbled.

Suddenly a young woman came rushing into the crowd and shouted, "Have mercy on me, Son of David; my daughter is tormented by a demon!" I knew she was a Canaanite because I recognized her accent. The young Rabbi said nothing—silence. Some of the surrounding men, I think disciples, said, "Send her away! She is bothering us—crying and shouting." The Rabbi looked at her and said, "I was sent only to the lost sheep of the house of Israel." I thought she would turn away, but instead she came and knelt at his feet: "Lord, help me." I thought for a moment that he was going to reach out and touch her. In fact, I was amazed that he even spoke to her since speaking to women, especially unfamiliar women, was frowned upon.

Then he said, "It is not fair to take the children's food and give it to the little dogs." Amazingly, this did not offend her, but seemed to inspire her—they were playing a sort of game. "Yes, Lord" she said, "but even the little dogs eat the crumbs that fall from their master's table." The Rabbi smiled, and blessed her, saying, "Woman, great is your faith. Let it be done for you as you wish." The woman began to cry and thanked the Rabbi and turned and ran back down the road.

I continued on toward Tyre. I couldn't help but wonder whether the woman's daughter was healed. I decided it was impossible that this young Rabbi had such power and that he had said this to her just to make her feel better and to give her some kind of hope. I arrived at my uncle Judah's house and they were all surprised to see me, but were glad for the offer of help. My cousins were much younger, so they needed my strong back to lift the stone. One wall had collapsed after a heavy rain and had to be rebuilt, and the roof needed repairs. We worked together the rest of the day, finally getting the walls in place and ready for the new roof, which would be the simple part. As we were cleaning up and washing away the dust and dirt from our bodies, a woman came to the door asking for my aunt. She said she had some amazing news. She and my aunt spoke loud enough for us all to hear. Apparently a young woman in the village had a daughter who had been tormented by a demon. She would suddenly cry out and jump around uncontrollably. This morning, her mother had gone to seek the help of a healer, and when she came home, the daughter was asleep and calm. She waited all day for the demon to attack her, but it never happened. She was healed. My aunt asked who this healer was. The other woman said she only knew that he was a Rabbi from Capernaum, a Rabbi Yeshua. I was stunned, and troubled, and said nothing of what I had seen. I had to find him again. I was ready to join him.

Sarah of Capernaum

SOMETIMES I THINK MY husband has lost his mind. I think he and his brother John both tossed their brains overboard in the middle of the Sea—along with their common sense. First, he becomes good friends with the new Rabbi. Then he tells me he is one of his disciples, along with Simon and Andrew, and, of course, brother John—they are now up to twelve men. He came in laughing the other night and told me that the Rabbi has given him and John a nickname: "Boanerges"—Sons of Thunder. He sounded like a 12-year-old. Now he tells me he has quit his job as a fisherman. They are all going to go off on missions in the countryside—maybe even to Jerusalem. "We are going to preach good news to the poor," he said. I said that he didn't have to go far to find the poor—just look at his own family and village. He said he was serious—they were all serious. Rabbi Yeshua has a vision of a new Israel, a new life, a new world. I had to admit that I have been impressed with his preaching and his gentle way with children. I know what he has done for Simon's mother-in-law and many in Capernaum and the countryside. He is an amazing healer. That's for sure. But these are uncertain times with the Roman occupation, the Zealot rebellion, all the taxes. And then there are all the purity restrictions by the Pharisees: don't do this, don't touch that, wash this, cleanse that. As if we don't have enough to do. At least we still have quiet Sabbath time. And now this hair-brained notion of a message of good news.

The next day I spent time with some women in the village: Simon's wife; Mary, Rabbi Yeshua's mother; Naomi, Nathaniel's wife; and Salome, the butcher's daughter. We devised a plan. When James came home, I told him I had talked with some other women and we have a plan: we are coming with you. Before he could say a word, I said to him: "So who is going to cook for you? And who is going to wash and mend your robes? And who is going to rub your big, bony feet when you come home at night?" He looked shocked; then sat down with his mouth open. I continued: "Some of us met and talked and we decided that Nathaniel's wife, Naomi, and Salome, the butcher's daughter, and, of course I, will go with you. We can't ask Simon's wife to go; she has children and an ailing mother. Your sister has to take care of your parents. And most of the other women have children or couldn't handle a bunch of foolish men." I almost laughed at his silence, but just kept chopping vegetables for dinner. Finally, he said, "I will have to talk with Rabbi Yeshua first. But I think it will be alright. In fact, I think it is a good idea." I knew he would not disagree with me. I had to prepare myself for when John, the other "Son of Thunder," hears about this. He will not be so easily convinced.

I put down my knife and went over and massaged James' shoulders. I know he wants to do what Rabbi Yeshua is asking of him. I know he wants to be a good and faithful Jew. I also know that he is choosing a hard path, a risky path, even a dangerous path. There are many who do not agree with what Rabbi Yeshua preaches. Many of the Pharisees see him as a threat to their teachings and their authority over the villagers and the synagogues. In fact, Mary told us that some of the older Rabbis came to her to ask her to speak with her son and ask him to be less radical in his views on the Torah and the traditions. They also recommended that he get married and raise a family. Mary told us women that she already has several grandchildren, but does not expect to have any from Yeshua. She said, "He is convinced that he will risk his life too often to ask any woman to marry him." Her eyes teared up when she told us that. James let out a long sigh and lowered his head. I slapped him on the back and said, "Now get yourself cleaned up for dinner. You smell like fish!"

Mathathias the Leper

BEGIN WAS A LOT easier when I had leprosy. Not that I want it back again, but people could see my disease, so they were more generous. Since I have been cured, most people just shrug and turn away or tell me to get a job. But now I think I have enough money to buy the sacrifices in the Temple. Now I can go to the priest and he can give me the blessing that I am clean—no longer a leper. I have several denarii and one good Roman coin given to me by a kind woman on the road to Jerusalem. The only problem is now I will have to go to the money-changers in the Temple and will probably get ripped off since I have to change it for Jewish money. One of these days some brave and righteous soul is going to throw those crooks out of the Temple. All I know is that somebody is getting paid off. Like the rest of life, "It's all rigged." as my uncle used to say. The Sadducees say that Roman coins are "unclean"—they have no idea what it means to be "unclean."

I was "unclean" for over ten years until my miracle happened. I had been a camel driver on the road between Jerusalem and Damascus. I don't know where I picked it up, but somewhere in my travels I came in contact with another leper. It might have been from infected baggage or a camel blanket—I don't know. All I remember is beginning to itch and scratch a lot. No amount of salve or washing helped. I tried to hide it, but soon it became too obvious that I had leprosy. I lost my job, my friends, any hope of ever getting married. Even my own family had to shun me. I could no longer play with my nieces and nephews, no longer visit my grandparents for dinner, no longer join my family for Shabbat meals and celebrations. It was like I was dead—alive—but dead. Old friends would just look past me. Women would ignore me. Even my rabbi shook his head when I came too close. I was "unclean" and could no longer be a part of the synagogue. I am sure that people were wondering what I had done to deserve God's punishment of leprosy. I am sure people said things like: "Well, you know those

78

camel drivers—they are always visiting whores up in Damascus." Or "Too many of these young men like to gamble in those dirty inns along the road." Or maybe they thought I took bribes or spied for the Romans. Well, they would all be wrong. I was honest and upright and clean—until I became "unclean." I would often pray to Adonai, asking why this had happened to me. What had I done to deserve this disease? I am ashamed to admit it, but sometimes I even cursed at him because I was so frustrated at being left out of society and family and even religion. I would challenge Adonai: "If you wanted me to be a good Jew, to be faithful and righteous, then why did you do this to me? Why me?"

For almost ten years, I had wandered up and down the roads of Israel. I went from my home in Galilee to Jerusalem. Then I went south to the Negev and then to Gaza and up the coast to Joppa and then back toward Galilee. If people only knew how lonely I was. By then I had joined up with two other lepers, so we kept watch over each other. But I was still lonely. Even the Samaritans wanted nothing to do with us. They laughed at us and taunted us with shouts of "Why don't you go to Jerusalem to be healed? Leave our towns!" As in most villages, the children would throw stones at us and men would yell at us to keep away from their homes. Sometimes the women would give us some water from a well and even some food—bread and fruit. One day near the village of Nain, a woman told us we should go toward the Sea of Gennesaret and ask for Rabbi Yeshua from Capernaum. She said he is a great healer and has great compassion. We thanked her and set out for the Jordan Valley.

We walked north and asked people if they knew of Rabbi Yeshua. Many just walked, even ran, away. Others told us to keep moving north, look for crowds of people. We walked further and were coming close to the Sea when we saw a large group of people in a field. As we approached, they moved aside, picking up their children and telling us to go away. My two friends stopped, but I continued on. Seated on a mound of grassy earth was a young man surrounded by eight or ten other young men. He looked at me and smiled. Then he motioned for me to come closer; so I did. When I was about ten feet away from him, I knelt down and said, "If you choose, you can make me clean." He smiled at me and said, "I do choose. Come closer." I scuttled closer to him and then he reached out his hand and touched me— one of the young men cried out, "Master! No!" But Rabbi Yeshua put both hands on my head and said, "Be clean!" Then he grasped my hands and arms and shoulders and said again, "Be clean!" I did not know what to do, so I cried. I had forgotten how wonderful it felt to be touched by another human being. I wanted to hug him but was afraid. I felt different. My entire body felt alive again. I don't know why, but I felt clean again. Through my tears, I thanked him again and again.

As I stood to go, he said to me, "Say nothing to anyone about this. Go to the priest and show yourself to him to be examined. Then make the sacrifice that Moses commanded for your cleansing." I said that I would and then turned to leave. I could not help myself. I returned to my friends and said, "Look at me! I'm healed! I am clean!" and they shook their heads in disbelief. As I walked along the path, everyone I met I told my story: ten years a leper and now I am clean. I praised Adonai and told how Rabbi Yeshua of Capernaum had touched me—actually touched a leper—and made me clean. I told everyone how I was going to go to Jerusalem, make sacrifice, and give testimony to the miracle of healing.

Now I am ready to go up to Jerusalem for the examination and make the sacrifice. I know I disobeyed him, but I had to tell the world what had happened to me. One traveler told me that my story had been re-told throughout Galilee and now Rabbi Yeshua could not enter a town without a mob forming. He had to stay out in the countryside with his disciples for fear of starting a riot. When I get to Jerusalem, I will tell everyone, including the Sadducees, about my miracle and the power of Rabbi Yeshua. I am sure they will be happy to hear that there is such a powerful healer in the land.

Tamar of Judah

THE REASON I LOVE him is that I have never been able to seduce him. I know it sounds strange, but it is true. He respects me. He refuses to use me. He loves me in a way I have never been loved before. He sees me as a woman, not as a piece of property or somehow of less worth than—well—than a man. It is hard to explain. Also, he has a sense of humor. He reminds me of my mother in some strange way. She had a sense of humor, too. She named me Tamar—after the woman in the Torah who "played the harlot" in order to achieve justice from one of the Patriarchs. Of course, she had no idea that I would become a real harlot playing for lots of patriarchs. It was Judah, I think, who gave her a ring as a pledge or payment. I, too, have received lots of rings and other gifts, not so much as pledges, but as payment for my services. But not from him.

My life had not been easy. I was the youngest of six children. Two of my brothers and my father died of some plague or illness that came to our village. My mother tried to keep our small farm going, but the drought ruined our crops for two years in a row. Another brother and a sister ran away to Damascus to live with relatives. That left my mother and a sister and me to fend for ourselves. I was very beautiful and attracted a lot of attention in the marketplace. One day an older man offered me food and wine if I came to his home and "entertained" him. We were desperate, so I said "Yes." I never told my mother what I had done and soon I was bringing home food and wine several times a week. She never asked.

After several months of visits to this older man's house, I arrived to find two other men waiting for me. They told me they wanted me to "entertain" them also, and if I refused, they would tell my family and make a public scandal of what I was doing. I believed I had no choice, so I agreed. It wasn't long before more men knew about me, and finally my mother was told by a neighbor. She was crushed and so was I. She had no choice but to disown me and, so, here I am—on my own—a big reputation, and a good business; and then this handsome rabbi shows up and invites me to have supper with him and some of his friends.

I was glad for the company—it all seemed so normal. I thought he would choose some quiet, hidden place, somewhere "discreet" as they say. But his choice was right out in the open, in a very public venue. I could tell that some of his friends were uncomfortable, but Rabbi Yeshua was not at all. He introduced me to the circle of men and concluded by welcoming a man named Matthew. He told the others, "This is Matthew. He had been a tax collector. But now he is one of us—a disciple for the Kingdom of Adonai—living proof that our Lord feasts on mercy not purity." As he said this, he looked at me and smiled. I blushed for the first time in years.

I went into hiding for a few days. I was confused and torn between changing my life and going back to my very lucrative profession. It would have been simple enough to just forget about that Rabbi—but I could not. I was in love—or so I thought. As I was struggling with what to do, there was a knock at my door. I assumed it was a "customer." When I opened the door, it was Rabbi Yeshua. My first thought was, "Now is my chance." He asked if he could come in, and I stood aside and welcomed him with a great smile. I closed the door and went to my bed and removed my shawl and loosened my hair. He simply said, "I have missed you at the marketplace and wanted to speak with you." I said, "I have missed you, too. I am so glad you came to see me." I sat down on the edge of the bed—a move that I knew so well. He looked at me and said, "You are a very attractive woman." He stepped toward me and I thought, "Now I have him." He placed his hand on my head and said, "I know what you expect from most men. But I am not most men. I have been called by Adonai for a purpose that will end in an early death. Therefore, I will not marry, nor will I be a father." I cried as I embraced his legs. "Do not be ashamed. And do not give up hope for a future. Adonai, and I, will not abandon you. You may join our band of disciples, or you may remain here in this village as an example of Adonai's mercy and love."

I released my grip, and he bent over to kiss me on the top of my head. He turned to leave, and I reached for a small bag of coins. I stood up and held them out to him. He smiled and said, "Give it to the poor and the hungry—there are many in need." He opened the door and stepped into the sunlight. "We will be leaving tomorrow for another village. Preaching good news and healing keeps us busy." As he walked away, I knew I was in love—but with whom and for what, I was not sure.

Judas Iscariot

MY GRANDMOTHER WAS THE one who first got me interested in the coming of "Messiah." She was blind and said she saw things that normal people could not see. She had dreams and visions and would quote the prophets— her favorite was Zechariah, or was it Malachi. My grandfather had died when I was a child. He had planted many vineyards and fruit trees in the mountainous terrain, and now my father and brothers continued to keep them strong. Our family is especially proud of our Judean dates, which even the Herods will pay a good price to serve at their banquets. My grandmother kept telling me that her husband had hoped to see the coming of Messiah and the restoration of the Kingdom of David. His last words, according to my grandmother, were from the Psalms: "Posterity shall serve Adonai; future generations shall be told about Adonai, and proclaim his deliverance to a people yet unborn, saying that Adonai has done it." He was a devout Jew who passed on his hopes to his wife and family. My grandmother was the one who told me to go to Qumran, where the people awaited the Messiah. "Don't go to Jerusalem," she said. "They are all disciples of Beelzebul—they lie and cheat and get rich on the backs of the poor—remember what Amos said," pointing her finger into the air for emphasis: "'I hate, I despise your festivals, and I take no delight in your solemn assemblies . . . But let justice roll down like waters, and righteousness like an ever-flowing stream.'" Then she added, "Go to Qumran on the Dead Sea—there you will find life." My father discouraged me. He said I would only find trouble and disappointment. I would do better to use my skill with numbers and accounts as a steward with a wealthy trader or farmer. Qumran was close to Kerioth, our village south of Hebron. It is just as far to go there as it is to go to Jerusalem, so I told my father that I was going to go to Jerusalem to look for work. I did not tell him I was also going to visit Qumran and find out more about the prophecies about Messiah.

I stopped in Hebron and went to the synagogue near the tomb of Abraham. I asked the rabbi about the people at Qumran and he shook his head and said they should be left alone. Then he laughed and said that they try to be even more pure than us Pharisees. When I did not laugh with him, he went back into the synagogue. I had wanted to ask him about the coming of Messiah but did not get the chance. I moved on toward Bethlehem and paused near ancient Tekoa, the home of Amos, the prophet. He and my grandfather would have understood each other since both farmed sycamore figs and both looked for the justice and wrath of Adonai. I soon passed the Fortress of Herodium and then began the deep descent to the Dead Sea. It was a tough road with few travelers. When I came near to Qumran, there were several tent camps with people sitting in what little shade there was. The heat was intense and the smell of the acrid salts was strong.

As I approached, I was hailed by a well-dressed man who asked me if I was a member of the community. I told him I was not but was interested in their teachings. I was particularly interested in Messiah. He nodded and smiled. "We are all waiting. We are all watching." He then told me I would have to speak to the Teacher of Righteousness before I could be part of the community. He invited me to stay with his family until I could be examined. "Examined?" I said. "By whom—and about what?" The man frowned at me and said, "You have to be pure enough—holy enough—and willing to give up your worldly goods." "But I am only interested in finding out more about the coming of Messiah. I don't want to become a disciple." He frowned even harder and turned away. He walked several paces and then turned back and said, "You are not ready for this place. But come and stay the night in our tent." I followed along, glad my father was not here to say, "I told you so." After a simple meal and long prayers and silence, the women gathered the dishes, and the men went outside into the now dark night. My host said that the one good thing about the sea salt was that it kept the insects away. He was a wealthy trader from Joppa on the coast, but had left his business to pursue the purity of the desert and found the Essenes of Qumran. He had been waiting months for the final decision that would allow him to enter the community. He was silent for a time and then suggested that if I was so interested in the coming of Messiah, I might do better by seeking John the Baptizer. He told me that John had been a member of the community at Qumran but had left in order to announce the coming of Messiah to Israel and to baptize for the forgiveness of sins. He had become very popular and was not far from here—near Jericho at last report.

In the morning I began walking the 10 miles to Jericho. I hoped to find John nearby, but was informed that he was farther north. "Just follow the Jordan Valley and look for a crowd," I was told. Luckily, I found the crowd just a few miles past Jericho's last orchards. There were about 40 people standing on the bank of the Jordan, men and women and even a few Roman soldiers in the back of the crowd. They were listening to a man who was standing waist deep in the river. He was dark-skinned, from the sun no doubt, and was wearing some kind of animal skin shirt. He kept lowering his hands into the water and then lifting handfuls and letting it run down his arms. As I came closer, I could hear him haranguing the people: "Why are you here! Who warned you to flee the wrath of Adonai? If you think being a child of Abraham is enough to save you, think again! Adonai can raise up children of Abraham from these stones. Bear fruit worthy of repentance. Right now, the ax is ready at the roots of the trees of Israel—every tree that does not bear good fruit will be cut down and thrown into the fire."

Someone on the bank of the river cried out, "What should we do?" John said, "Whoever has two coats must give one to someone who has none. If you have food, you must share it with the hungry." John raised his hand and pointed to two men: "And you tax collectors, take only what is lawful for you to collect." One soldier called out, "How about us? What should we do?" John frowned and said, "Do not threaten people and extort money with violence. Do not lie and be satisfied with your wages." Finally, someone asked, "Are you the Messiah?" John raised his hands full of water and shouted, "No! I baptize you with water—for repentance. But there is one coming who is more powerful than I am; I am not worthy to untie his sandals. This one will baptize you with the Holy Spirit and with fire. The harvest is coming—the wheat will be gathered into Adonai's barn, the chaff," and then he paused, "will be burned with unquenchable fire."

People entered the river to be baptized. I was stunned and unable to move. I kept thinking, "If John is not the Messiah, then who is? And where can I find this one?

Rufus of Gerasa

SOME PEOPLE ARE STILL afraid of me. I don't blame them. I was a scary, crazy, violent person for many years. I am no longer that person. I am a preacher of peace and mercy, of the coming kingdom of Adonai, and a follower of Messiah—Rabbi Yeshua of Capernaum. I don't remember when it all started, I mean, when my world began to fall apart. I was born into a Jewish family near Gerasa, part of the Decapolis—the Ten Cities—a collection of Greek cities east of the Jordan River, an independent region of the Roman Empire. We were important on the trade routes and were not ruled by any of the Herods or even a Roman governor. My family was settled and prosperous. Since we lived on the Sea of Galilee, we often traveled across to visit the Jewish communities in Capernaum and Tiberias and even to Sepphoris. All of that stopped when my demons appeared.

It got so bad that I had to leave my home, and my town, and my friends. The people were so afraid of me that they made me live in the tombs on the outside of the town. My parents and some friends would bring me food and water, but I threatened them so often that they chained me to some rocks. That didn't work because I easily broke the chains. I didn't realize it then, but people would come from far away to see the "Gerasene Demoniac." People would even pay to be brought out to the tombs to watch me break the chains and throw rocks and scream and moan. Over the years my demons multiplied, and I lost all sense of what it meant to be human, much less religious. Most of my life as an adult I could not remember. I had to hear about it from my mother and my sisters who had cared for me while I was possessed. It was from them that I also learned about my release at the hands of Rabbi Yeshua.

One day a fishing boat arrived at the town and Rabbi Yeshua and some of his disciples came ashore. They had heard about me from some other fishermen and tried to heal me. They came to the tombs and I must have frightened some disciples with my chains and screams, for they backed away and stood at a distance. Then one of them came forward, and my demons cried out when they saw him. They must have known who he was—as I have come to know him—Adonai's Messiah. They cried out, "What do you want with us?" He asked, "What is your name?" They answered, "If we tell you, then you will have power over us." Rabbi Yeshua raised his voice and demanded, "Tell me your name!" They replied, "Legion, for we are many, very many. But do not cast us out into the abyss, into chaos! Let us go into that herd of pigs! The ones over there." I am told that Rabbi Yeshua allowed them to leave me and go into the pigs. My mother told me that as soon as that happened, the herd ran down the hill and over the cliff and drowned in the sea. The pig herders were furious and frightened and right away ran into the city to report what had happened.

Soon people from the city were coming out to see what had happened. All of them were amazed to see me sitting on one tomb, quiet and in my right mind, conversing with Rabbi Yeshua. Some were thankful and praised Adonai. But others were angry because they had made money bringing visitors to the tombs to see the "Mad Man of Gerasa." Many were simply afraid of the power that Rabbi Yeshua displayed, and they asked him to leave. The herders of the pigs were the most upset since they had lost their entire livelihood. I looked for my parents, who were in the crowd, but were wary of coming too close. I never found a home again with them. My demons had made them too afraid, and they had other children—my brothers and sisters who I would slowly come to know and love. One great irony of all of this was that I ended up living with one of the pig herders—imagine a Jewish man living with pig herders. Fortunately, they have been able to regain another herd of pigs.

At the end of that fateful day, Rabbi Yeshua and his disciples were preparing to leave in their boat, and I begged him to let me come with him. I stood knee deep in the water, holding on to the gunnel of the boat. He turned to me and said, "Stay here with your people and proclaim how much Adonai has done for you. Proclaim the good news of the coming Kingdom, share the same mercy shown to you with all you meet." I was sad to see him leave, but I knew that I now had a story to tell and a life to give to Adonai and my brothers and sisters in the Decapolis. I even helped push the boat out into deeper water.

Simeon of Anathoth

I AM A LAWYER, devoted to the Torah, tasked with the duty of interpreting the traditions of my people in a world of threats and challenges and choices. Lawyers sometimes get a terrible reputation. We are charged with always splitting hairs, always arguing over minute points of obscure instruction, accused of making life difficult—as if life were not difficult enough without us. We are asked to rule on serious cases involving divorce, and property, and liability, and inheritance. We are also asked to rule on minor issues of dress, and table manners, and diet, and on and on and on. Our tradition is to have debate and discussion in public so that ordinary people can hear and learn and follow Torah.

Recently I learned of a young Rabbi from Capernaum in Galilee—a certain Yeshua—who was attracting a lot of attention with his teachings and stories. He was famous as a healer and miracle worker. I was intrigued. I finally met him in a small village south of Tiberias, on the Jordan Valley road. He was engaged in telling some stories, some parables, to the people gathered around him. I listened for a while and was impressed with his grasp of the prophets and the promises of life everlasting. I stood up and asked him, "Teacher, what must I do to inherit eternal life?" He looked deeply at me, even into me. Then he asked me, "What is written in the Torah? What do you read there?" I smiled knowingly, and replied, "You shall love your Lord, Adonai, with all your heart, and with all your soul, and with all your strength, and with all your mind; and you shall love your neighbor as yourself." He smiled back at me and said, "You are right. Do this and you will live."

He was about to go on, when I asked him, "And who is my neighbor?" The young Rabbi paused and then asked me, "Do you know the road from Jerusalem down to Jericho?" I said, "Yes. It is a difficult and sometimes dangerous way." He nodded and continued, "Well, one day there was a

man going down that road. Suddenly a group of thieves sprang from behind some rocks and threw him to the ground and stripped him of his
clothes and belongings, and beat him, and left him for dead. Now by chance
a priest was going down that road. But when the priest saw the man, he
passed by on the other side of the road. Soon a Levite, too, came down the
road. And he, likewise, passed by on the other side. But then a Samaritan
was travelling on the road, and when he saw the man left for dead he was
moved with pity. He went to the man and bandaged his wounds, pouring
on oil and wine. Then the Samaritan picked him up, put him on his own
donkey, brought him to an inn, and took care of him. The next morning,
he gave the innkeeper two denarii and said, 'Look after this man and when
I come back, I will pay you for whatever more you spend.'" The young
Rabbi paused, looked at the crowd, then at me and asked, "Now, which of
these three do you think was a neighbor to this man who was robbed and
beaten?" I could tell that I was flushed. Everyone was looking at me. Then
I quietly said, "The one who showed him mercy." Rabbi Yeshua said to me,
"Go and do likewise."

I wanted to argue with him. I wanted to tell him that the priest had
to maintain his purity in order to serve in the Temple and therefore could
not touch a dead person without defiling himself and making his service
impossible. I wanted to tell him that the Levite, too, could not touch blood
without making himself unclean and therefore unable to fulfill his duties. I
wanted to tell him that purity was important, that the Torah is clear about
these things. But, in the end, I had to choose mercy over purity. I could
have been angry. I could have felt that he had tricked me. But I didn't. I felt
relieved. I felt unburdened. I felt I had a new insight into the Torah and the
prophets. And I had a problem—a big problem. How could I tell my col-
leagues that our way of reading Scripture was not so simple? How could I
continue to make rulings and give advice without knowing more about the
people who would be affected and their situation in life? How could I go on
without challenging the Scribes and Pharisees who have so much power? I
did not have the answers, but I did have the questions—so many questions.

Mary of Magdala

THE FIRST TIME I saw him was on the beach near Magdala where I live. He and his disciples had come ashore to cook a meal. Someone knew him, this young Rabbi from Capernaum, and spread the word. Soon there was a small crowd of people asking for healing for several sick and lame members of the village. I watched as he and his disciples cared for the people and actually healed them. I had been warned about him by Rabbi Eliezar in Tiberias. Magdala is too small for our own synagogue, and Tiberias is a Sabbath's walk north, so we travel there for worship and teaching. Rabbi Eliezar had told us that the rabbi from Capernaum is to be shunned because his teachings are not in accordance with the Torah, and in fact were dangerous. My ears perked up when he said that he even accepts women as disciples.

Before long, some of the local Pharisees showed up to challenge Rabbi Yeshua. They taunted him, asking, "Show us a sign from heaven to prove that what you are doing is from Adonai." Rabbi Yeshua came up to them and said, "Do you know the saying, 'Red sun at night—sailors delight. Red sun in the morning—sailors take warning?'" They said, "Yes, of course we know that." Yeshua said, "So you know how to interpret the signs of the skies, but you do not know how to interpret the signs of the times." Then he frowned at them and said, "Only a faithless generation asks for a sign. And you will get none except the sign of Jonah." With that he turned to his disciples and they all got into their boats and sailed away to the east. I was stunned and could not suppress a smile as the Pharisees shook their heads in puzzlement and went away mumbling. I had to learn more about this startling young man.

Several weeks later, I had traveled north to Caesarea Philippi to visit my sister who had just given birth. Her husband serves in the palace of King Philip. Since I had some wealth, my travel, though long, was not uncomfortable. I had married outside the Jewish religion, an older man, a Gentile

90

from the Decapolis who was a trader in figs, dates, and other goods. When he died, I moved back to Magdala. I was still quite young, and I had learned a lot from my husband, so I continued to direct the business in trade. I am always amazed at how wealth covers a multitude of sins. My hometown neighbors forgave my youthful rebelliousness, and I was welcomed back into the synagogue—for a price, of course. I was always embarrassed when Rabbi Eliezar made a public display of a gift I had given to the synagogue.

While I was in Caesarea Philippi, I heard that Rabbi Yeshua from Capernaum was also in the area. One morning I walked out onto the trade route and asked for his whereabouts. No one knew where he was until I saw two of his disciples. I recognized them from that day on the beach. I asked them where Rabbi Yeshua was. They looked at me with suspicion. They were probably not used to a woman alone, asking questions of them in public. "Why do you ask?" one of them said. I told them I had heard his discussion with the Pharisees in Magdala and I wanted to ask him about the "sign of Jonah." I didn't understand what he meant. The other disciple laughed and said, "There is a lot that he says that people don't understand." The other disciple added, "Yes. At first people do not understand because he speaks in parables—he tells stories. He wants us to think for ourselves. He wants us to figure out what we are to do for the kingdom and then do it—not just talk about it." The first disciple shook his head, "The kingdom of Adonai is like a mustard seed, the kingdom is like leaven in a loaf, like salt, like finding a lost coin or a lost sheep—or a lost child. I know sometimes I feel lost." I smiled and asked again where Rabbi Yeshua was. The first disciple pointed north and said, "He took three of the disciples and went up on the mountain. Probably to pray—he is always praying." The other disciple smiled and said, "Bartholomew does not like to pray a lot. But the Rabbi should be back soon. There are people waiting for him, waiting to be healed." He pointed down the road to a group of ten or twelve people sitting in the shade. "There is a man there with his son, who falls down and goes rigid and foams at the mouth. We tried to heal him but could not. He will have to wait for Rabbi Yeshua." I thought I would wait too.

Shortly before noon, we saw a group of men coming from the north, from Mt. Hermon. Someone shouted, "He's coming! He's coming down the road! He will help us!" The group that had been waiting quickly ran into the road and moved to meet the Rabbi and his disciples. Leading the group was a man carrying a young boy who was thrashing around. They yelled at the disciples, who yelled back at them. Rabbi Yeshua stepped between them, then asked his disciples, "What are you arguing about with the people?" The man holding the boy answered, "I brought my son to be healed, but they could not help us. He falls down and goes rigid and foams at the mouth. What am I to do?" Rabbi Yeshua looked angrily at his disciples: "You faithless generation! How much longer do I have to put up with you? Bring the boy to me." Then he asked the father, "How long has this been happening?" The father said, "Since he was a child. Sometimes he throws himself around uncontrollably. One time he even fell into the fire, another time into deep water. Please help us!" Rabbi Yeshua said to the father, "All things are possible for one who believes." The father started to weep and cried out, "I believe; help my unbelief!" I said a quiet 'Amen' to that. Suddenly the boy began to convulse and fell to the ground, rolling around. Yeshua grabbed hold of the boy, closed his eyes, and looked to the heavens, his mouth moving ever so slightly. Then he shouted, "Come out of him! And never enter this boy again!" When he released him, the boy fell down as if dead, but Yeshua took him by the hand, lifted him up, and gave him to his father.

The circle of villagers and disciples were absolutely silent. The father wept over his now healthy son. I was again stunned by the power of this young man. The villagers rejoiced and sang praise to Adonai. One woman came forward and gave one disciple a sack of bread and olives. Another placed some fruit on the ground in front of Yeshua. They moved off to the south, smiling and looking back at the group of disciples and their Rabbi. I stood behind two tall men trying to be as inconspicuous as possible. One disciple asked Yeshua, "Why couldn't we heal the boy? We tried—we really did!" Yeshua smiled and said that this kind of spirit can only be cast out through prayer. Then he looked over at Bartholomew, who hung his head and said, "All right. All right. I will pray more often. I will even try to like it." The others laughed and slapped him on the shoulder. Yeshua continued, "And when you pray, do not look so sad or grimace like you were in pain. And don't heap up empty phrases like the Gentiles do. They think the more words you use, the more Adonai will listen. They do it so people will think they are so very religious—that is their reward. And don't pray loudly in public, on a street corner for everyone to see you. When you pray, go to a quiet place alone in secret, even into a closet, and Adonai will hear you in secret. You know Adonai knows your needs even before you ask."

I knew suddenly that Rabbi Yeshua had noticed me standing behind his disciples. As he came toward me, I realized that my heart was beating fast and I was strangely embarrassed. I felt like a very self-conscious young woman, but I was older than the Rabbi and a widow, and I wanted to run away. He looked at me—almost into me. "Who are you? If I may ask." I looked back at him and said, "I am Mary, from Magdala, near Tiberias. I am here visiting my sister, and I wanted to meet you." He replied, "And you have a question." "Yes," I said. "I want to know what you meant by 'the sign of Jonah.'" "The sign of Jonah?" He thought for a moment and then laughed, "Oh! You must have been there on the beach when I spoke with the Pharisees who wanted a sign." "Yes. I was. What did you mean?" He smiled and said, "Do you know the story?" "Yes. Of course. Every Jewish child knows the story of Jonah and the big fish and Nineveh." "Do you think it is funny? The story?" I thought for a moment, then said, "Well, yes, I suppose it is funny—Jonah getting all upset, angry because his preaching worked, and Nineveh repented." "Well, maybe 'the sign of Jonah' is to have a sense of humor. So many people take themselves far too seriously. With all their rules and prohibitions, they have no time to enjoy the beauty and the joy of the world and the people. They have made the Torah a burden, like a millstone around one's neck instead of a blessing and a joy." I nodded my head. He continued, "And you have another question." "Yes, I do," I said. "I hear you take women as disciples. I would like to become one." He looked into me again and then said, "You are welcome, Mary of Magdala. It will not be easy or without suffering, but you are welcome." Then he reached out with both of his hands and I placed mine in his. He squeezed tightly, then said, "In fact, we will need your help for our next journey—to Jerusalem." Once more I was stunned.

Bartholomew of Cana

I WAS NEVER VERY comfortable with the unexpected. As a farmer, I liked the ordinary, the predictable, the cycles of planting, nurturing, pruning, and harvesting. Becoming a follower of Yeshua was a real challenge for me. I was drawn to his charismatic preaching and the remarkable power of his healing, but it was his regular breaking of taboos that troubled me: he touched lepers and dead people; he spoke openly with prostitutes and sinners; and he broke sabbath rules, which caused a lot of problems with the Pharisees and local synagogue leaders. My home town of Cana is a pretty conservative place. I grew up in a strict household, which was fine with me since I liked structure and knowing what the rules were.

My older brother was getting married and there was to be a grand ceremony and a feast to follow. My father invited everyone he knew and a lot that he did not know. It was very unlike him, but this was his first son and he was eager to have grandchildren. It was at the wedding that I first met Rabbi Yeshua and some of his followers. My father had invited as many rabbis as he could find, so there was a lot of arguing going on much of the time. Rabbi Yeshua's mother was there too. I think she had been a friend of my mother's in Nazareth some years ago. Since I am somewhat shy and quiet, I was not in the middle of the party and the drinking—and there was a lot of drinking. In fact, there was a point where the wine was almost gone. I had gone to the storeroom to look for more when I overheard Rabbi Yeshua's mother telling him that there was no more wine. I looked in the storeroom but found none.

A few minutes later, the steward of the ceremony came out with huge vessels of wine and announced that the best wine had been saved for this time in the party. My father asked him where the wine had come from and the steward looked baffled and said, "It must have been hidden in the storeroom. None of the servants know where it came from."

Then he laughed and said, "It must be a miracle." And they both laughed and poured some more wine. I went back into the kitchen and asked one servant about the wine. He said, "I don't know. Ask the rabbi from Capernaum. " Then he shook his head and wouldn't say any more. I found one of his disciples, Simon of Capernaum, who told me that Rabbi Yeshua can not only change lepers into clean people, he can change water into wine. Then he looked at me with a smile and said, "Maybe he can change you from a farmer into a follower." He slapped me hard on the shoulder and said, "Now go have another cup of that delicious wine—and then come and join us."

I had trouble sleeping that night, so I wandered out into a nearby field where some partygoers were sleeping. I was looking for Simon. I found the disciples of Rabbi Yeshua, but Simon was asleep. His brother Andrew told me I dare not wake him: "He is a bear when he is wakened before sunrise." Then he asked me to sit down and said, "What did you want to ask him?" I said that I wanted to ask him if the rumor was true. Had Rabbi Yeshua changed the water in the jars into wine? I wanted to know how he had done it and if the other stories about him healing people were also true. And I wanted to know why all of you are following him. What do you want to happen? I stopped before I appeared foolish.

Andrew nodded his head and said, "Rabbi Yeshua is here to announce the coming of the Kingdom of Adonai. Do you know about Messiah—the anointed one?" I said, "Yes." "Well, we are convinced that Rabbi Yeshua is the one will bring in this kingdom—not what we thought, though. He preaches a message of mercy, rather than purity—the kingdom will be open to all people, not just the pious and law-abiding. It will be filled with lepers and sinners and lame and outcasts. And I hope you are shocked by that, because all of us were." I was more than shocked—I was speechless. "But how will you do it? How will this all take place?" Andrew sighed and said, "I don't know. I just know that we have come to have faith in him. He often speaks in parables. One day he said, 'The kingdom of Adonai is as if a farmer would scatter seed on the ground and then go home and sleep and rise night and day, and the seed would sprout and grow, he does not know how. The earth produces—first the stalk, then the head, then the full grain. And then the harvest when the grain is ripe, he goes in with his sickle because the harvest has come. We plant the seed—the harvest will come when the time is ready. He told another parable about the mustard seed, the smallest seed, but when it is planted and grown to its fullest, it is the largest of the trees and all kinds of birds make their nests in it." He paused, then said, "What do you think? Are you with us?" For once in my life, I did not hesitate—I said, "Yes! I am with you."

Elishat of Tyre

I DREADED THE MORNINGS because it meant I had to leave my daughter alone while I went to carry water. At least she was sleeping now. Most of the night she tossed and turned and cried out several times, waking the neighbor's dogs. I fear the demon will return as soon as I leave the house. It has been two weeks, and I am exhausted. I have no more tears and no more prayers. As I was looking for my water jugs, there was a knock at the door. "Come in," I cried with little hospitality. "You know I cannot come into your house, under your roof," said a gentle voice. It was my Jewish neighbor Zipporah. "Oh. Of course," I said. "Sorry. I didn't know it was you." "How is your daughter?" she asked. "Right now, she is sleeping. But any moment she could be possessed again and . . . and . . . and I do not know what to do." My knees went weak, and I had to sit down. "Will you watch her while I go to get water?" I asked. "I think it would be better if I went to get your water. But you know it will take longer because I will have to wait at the end of the line until all the other women fill their jugs. At least they still allow Jews to use the same well. In other places we have to go out of the villages to get water." I stood back up and handed her my two jugs through the door. "I will be back as soon as I can," she said.

Over an hour later, Zipporah returned with the water. She was also very excited about something and fidgeted nervously as she passed me the jugs through the open door. "What is wrong?" I asked. She pressed her hands together and said, "At the well, I was talking to another Jewish woman from the village and she told me something that might help you." She paused, and I said, "Well, go on." She began, "I know you are not Jewish, but I will tell you, anyway. My friend was just at a wedding in Cana, in Galilee, you know, part of Israel, and she told me about a young rabbi from Capernaum—one Yeshua. Well, there was a great crowd for the wedding and the feast, and they were about to run out of wine. Then, there suddenly

97

appeared large jars filled with wonderful wine and nobody knew where it came from. My friend overheard some servants saying that the rabbi from Capernaum had changed their water into this amazing wine." I looked at her and said, "So, how is this going to help me and my daughter?" Zipporah continued: "My friend found the rabbi's mother and spoke with her—one Mary from Nazareth—and she said that her son had amazing powers. He has cured leprosy, and make blind people see again and the lame walk," and she paused, "and best of all—he casts out demons. And, he is coming to Tyre—he wants to see the home of Jezebel." Then I said, "Yes, but I am not Jewish." "Oh, I don't think that will matter. Just address him as 'Son of David' since some people think he is the Messiah. And ask, beg even, for your daughter. He should be easy to find since he is traveling with twelve young men, and his mother and some women." I decided to take a chance.

My daughter was sleeping, a little restless, but sleeping when I left her. Zipporah said she would sit outside the door and call a neighbor if my daughter became unsettled. I began to walk to the main road and kept thinking about what I would say. Over and over in my mind, I rehearsed how to address this rabbi. I was desperate. I had to believe that she could be healed and that this Jewish man could heal her. I had to have faith that the God of the Jews would have mercy on me. It wasn't long before I came upon a small group of people sitting in the shade by the side of the road. I somehow knew it was him, sitting in the middle of the group. I shouted, "Help me! Have mercy on me!" Then I remembered what Zipporah had told me, so I shouted again, "Lord, Son of David. Have mercy on me! My daughter is possessed by a demon!" I waited, but he did not say a word to me. Some of his followers said, "Send her away. She is so noisy and keeps shouting at us." Then the rabbi held up his hand to silence them. He looked at me and said, "I was sent only to the lost sheep of the house of Israel." I came closer and knelt in the dust: "Help me, please." He frowned and said, "It is not fair to take the children's food from the table and throw it to the little dogs." I thought I detected a slight smile, and said to myself, "He is playing a game with me—he is challenging me to answer." Then I said to him, "Yes, Lord. That is true. But even the little dogs eat the crumbs that fall from the master's table." Suddenly he smiled and laughed, saying, "Woman, great is your faith. Let it be done for you as you wish. Go in peace!" Then he looked at his followers, who were silent and shaking their heads. Only an older woman, maybe his mother, was smiling with tears in her eyes.

I turned and ran as fast as I could back to our village. Zipporah was standing outside my door with another neighbor, and they were talking and laughing. When they saw me, they came toward me, told me that a short time ago my daughter had awakened and called for me—she was hungry and wanted to know where you were. "She is cured! She is happy! She, she is herself again." Zipporah looked at me and whispered, "He did it, didn't he?" I smiled through my tears and said, "Yes."

Thaddeus of Nain

IT WAS AN EMBARRASSMENT. All of us who had stayed behind were totally embarrassed. We could not cast out a demon and cure a young boy. Rabbi Yeshua and the three favored ones, Simon and James and John, had all gone up the mountain to pray, or talk, or something. The rest of us were left here with the crowd, just waiting for something to happen. Suddenly this man comes charging into the middle of us demanding that we cure his son who was an epileptic. He screamed at us, "He falls to the ground. He falls into the fire or into the water. Help him!" And we tried. We prayed. We laid on hands and cried out. We lifted him up and I don't know what else. Nothing seemed to work. That is until Rabbi Yeshua arrived from the mountaintop. He asked us what was going on and so we told him about our failure to heal the boy. He wasn't pleased. He called us worthless and faithless and asked for the boy. Naturally, he was able to cure him. And, naturally, John made some snide remark, while James just smirked at us. At least Simon said nothing—just shook his head and frowned.

It is not easy being a disciple of this intense young Rabbi and his whirl-wind mission to save the world. He expects us all to be like him. But he is the Messiah, not us. The first time he sent us out to the nearby villages, we were able to do some good and powerful things. We preached and healed and gained a lot of followers. We returned to him very excited and even bragged about what we had done. He warned us not to be so proud, just to be glad that our names were written in the book of life. Another time, on one of our hikes, as we like to call them, we were comparing experiences trying to claim who was better than whom; who was the best at healing or preaching; or who could look a demon in the face and tell him to get lost. Rabbi Yeshua overheard us and asked us what we were talking about. We were ashamed to speak up. He waited until we were in the next village and he sat down with some little children and then called us to sit down with him. He took one of the little ones and said, "This child is perfect for the Kingdom of Adonai because there is nothing she can do to deserve it. Unless you receive the Kingdom like this little child, you shall not inherit it. If you want to be the greatest in the Kingdom," then he paused and looked at each of us in turn, "then you shall be a servant to all. If you want to be the biggest, you must be the smallest. Anyone who welcomes this child welcomes me. Anyone who rejects or hurts this little one, it is as if a millstone were placed around his neck and he were thrown into the sea." Then he tickled the little girl and sent her off.

As I said, it is not easy being one of his disciples. We have all been caught up in his vision of a new world, a new life, a new reality. We have literally left everything to follow him. Not just the twelve closest, but the women, too. For many of us, we have had to learn a whole new way of reacting to threats and insults and even violence, from both Romans and Zealots. We have been called names, accused of being disciples of Beelzebul. We have been ejected from synagogues and some of our own families have disowned us. In return, we have been asked to show love and mercy and forgiveness. We have been taught to be peaceful, even when struck in the face, or threatened with stoning. This has been especially tough for John and Simon, who had reputations as rough and tumble fishermen. Simon still carries a sword, but has never used it—at least not yet.

Rabbi Yeshua does not make it any easier for us when he disregards Sabbath laws, praises Samaritans, makes friends with prostitutes and tax collectors, and challenges the teachings of the Scribes and Pharisees, "blind guides" he calls them. And he is always making us think with his parables. Sometimes I get it and sometimes I just can't grasp what he is getting at. Like the one about the lost sheep. Any shepherd who has 99 sheep and one lost one would never leave the 99 in the wilderness—that is crazy. He should be glad that there is only one lost sheep. And the one about the workers in the vineyard where the owner pays them all the same even though some worked and sweated all day long and others only worked an hour or two. Paying them all the same just isn't fair. I do get the one about the three guys who are given some money to invest, and the one guy buries his. I get it that we all need to use our gifts and not be afraid to take a risk.

What worries me the most is where this is all headed. Rabbi keeps making more and more powerful enemies. And he is insistent on going up to Jerusalem again—the heart of his opposition. It does not help that he has already predicted his arrest and punishment and death, not just once but twice. He tells us he must go to Jerusalem, to the Temple, in order to proclaim the coming of the kingdom of Adonai and give to the people the chance to choose: repentance over pride, mercy over purity, life over death. If it does come to pass that he is killed, what will happen to us who have followed? Where shall we go? What will they do to us? What can we do in the face of all the power of Rome and the Temple?

Simon of Capernaum

ABOUT A WEEK AFTER it happened, John took me aside while the others were resting in the shade. "Did you tell anyone?" he asked. "No," I said. "Have you?" He looked at the others and said, "No. But I have wanted to tell someone." I grabbed his shoulder and said, "He told us strictly not to tell anyone. He must have his reasons. You know what he said: 'Whatever you do, do not tell anyone about what has happened on the mountaintop. If you tell them, they won't understand. Each of you has been given a vision of who I am and of Adonai's promise of a new world. Others will expect to experience it the same way, but they cannot. They will find it in a different way and at a different time. So do not tell anyone what has happened.'" John nodded in agreement, but I could tell he was still aching to tell someone.

It was all so strange and amazing. We had gone up the mountain, I assumed, to pray. Rabbi Yeshua and James and John and myself. I was always a little uncomfortable when he took the three of us apart from the others, but that was his choice. We got to the top, and I was tired from the climb, so I stretched out in the shade of a rock. Yeshua went to the highest point and looked out toward the west. James and John also sat down and soon we were all dozing. A cloud, or what we thought was a cloud, settled on the mountain and then we heard voices. We jumped up and there was Rabbi Yeshua and two other men—old men—I mean really old men. They were dressed funny and talked funny too. They were all talking together. I couldn't understand what they were saying, but the two older men seemed to be deferring to or honoring Yeshua. James, the smart one among us, said, "I know who they are: Moses and Elijah. Remember, Moses was buried, but no one could find his tomb, so it was assumed he had been taken to heaven by Adonai. And Elijah was carried away in a fiery chariot. Now they have come back. But why?" I remember saying, since I can never keep quiet, "Rabbi, it is good that we are here. We should make three tents—one for you and one for each of the others." I looked at James who said, "For Moses and Elijah—for the Torah and the Prophets." Rabbi Yeshua smiled at him. Suddenly the two old men disappeared and Rabbi Yeshua's robe was glowing, as if it were bleached as white as the sun. We all turned away and shielded our eyes. When we looked again, we saw only Rabbi Yeshua. Then, as the cloud got thicker, I am sure I heard a voice that said, "This is my son. Listen to him!" The others heard it, too.

We were all quiet on the way back down the mountain. It wasn't until we neared the bottom that Rabbi Yeshua told us not to tell anyone about what had happened, what we had seen and heard. He did say that we could tell of this vision only after the Son of Man is raised from the dead. This wasn't the first time he had told us to keep quiet about his identity. Not long before this mountaintop vision, we had been travelling with a crowd of people near Caesarea Philippi, and he had asked us who people thought he was—what they thought of him. We said that there was gossip that he was Elijah or one of the prophets. Others said he was John the Baptist come back to life—we laughed at that since this would have scared Herod Antipas half to death. We were all quiet when I spoke up and said, "You are Messiah, Adonai's anointed one." It was then that he told us not to tell anyone about him. While we were puzzled, he began to talk about how the Son of Man was going to be arrested and suffer greatly and be rejected by the elders and scribes in Jerusalem, and be killed, but in three days would rise from the dead. I knew he was talking about himself, so I grabbed him and took him aside and told him, "This will never happen to you. Not while I am around." He pushed me aside and said, loud enough for all to hear, "Get behind me, you tempter. You are thinking like a human, not as Adonai thinks." I remember being ashamed and hurt. I was only trying to protect him. I didn't yet get what his mission was.

He turned to the waiting crowd and began to preach: "If any one of you wants to become my follower, let them deny themselves and pick up their cross and follow me. Those who want to save their life will lose it, and those who lose their life for my sake and for the good news of the kingdom of Adonai," then he paused and looked at the crowd, "you will save your life. What will you profit to gain the whole world and lose your life? What can you give in exchange for your life? Any off you who are ashamed of me and my words in this adulterous and sinful generation, of you the Son of Man will be ashamed when he comes in the glory of Adonai and the holy angels." He paused and smiled at the crowd and then at us disciples: "Truly,

truly I tell you all, there are some here that will not taste death until you see the kingdom of Adonai come with power." It wasn't until much later that I would understand what that power was that he promised to some of us. I remember that sermon because it was then that I began to understand what he was up to and who he really was. Nevertheless, his mention of the cross gave me the shivers. I wouldn't wish that even on my worst enemy. For some time after this I was known as 'Simon the Tempter' and I had to endure the teasing because it was true.

Samuel of Capernaum

I WAS REALLY BORED. I kept digging into the dirt on the hillside, hoping to find something interesting, but so far, the only thing I had found were some ants and a few worms. There was a large beetle, but it jumped away before I could catch it. I had uncovered a few round stones which I wanted to throw at someone and knew I would be in trouble if I did. My parents were still listening to our rabbi tell stories. I have to admit he had great stories, and I liked them a lot, but he went on for too long. I especially like his camel jokes. One day he was arguing with another rabbi from Tiberias and finally told him, "You strain out a gnat and swallow a camel." Another time he was talking with a well-dressed man from Sepphoris when he told him, "It is easier for a camel to go through the eye of a needle than for a rich man to get into heaven." I really laughed at that one—imagine a big furry headed camel trying to poke through a tiny needle hole.

My uncle Andrew is one of Rabbi Yeshua's closest friends, so we get to hear a lot of what happens on their trips and adventures. They just got back from Tyre, where Rabbi healed the daughter of a Canaanite woman. I guess James and John made quite a fuss when she approached Rabbi Yeshua. They told her to keep quiet and go away. Uncle Andrew always gets upset when they overreact and get impatient. Rabbi Yeshua calls them "Boanerges," Sons of Thunder. I don't think it's a compliment. They had all gone to a wedding at Cana and then went on to Tyre so Rabbi could see the home of Jezebal. I guess they came back with a new follower, a farmer from Cana who joined the group. I am still bored. We had been here much of the day and I was getting hungry. I think I am the only one who brought some extra food along, and I am embarrassed to get it out when no one else has anything. I lay back on the grass and fell asleep.

I woke up when someone stepped on my leg. What was happening? Where did these people come from? There must be a thousand or more.

They were all milling around, trying to get close to Rabbi Yeshua, who was still talking. My uncle Andrew and the other disciples were trying to keep the crowd calm, but there were a lot of families with children who were whining. I crept closer and sat with my aunt Miriam. Rabbi Yeshua had called his disciples together. He told them that the crowd was hungry and needed to eat after being in the wilderness for such a long time. Simon asked, "Where can we find enough food to feed such a large crowd. There must be a few thousand people. Even if we went to the nearest town, we could not find enough." Rabbi Yeshua said, "I don't want to send them away hungry. How much food do we have?" They all looked at each other and shook their heads. I stood up and said, "I have seven small loaves of bread and a few fish." Uncle Andrew came and took them and gave them to Rabbi Yeshua. Miriam took her baby out of her basket and gave it to Simon. Several other women offered their baskets, too. Rabbi Yeshua took the loaves and looked to heaven and said a prayer. Then he broke the small loaves and the fish and put them in the empty baskets. Then he gave the baskets to the disciples and told them to offer the bread and fish to the crowd. The disciples looked at him in disbelief, but they began to walk through the crowd. People reached into the baskets and pulled out handfuls of bread and pieces of fish. There was almost a riot as people pushed in to get fed. I couldn't believe what was happening.

When the crowd had all gone away, Rabbi Yeshua said to his disciples, "Now collect all the leftovers. Nothing shall go to waste." Later, Uncle Andrew said to me they had collected twelve baskets full of bread and fish. Then he smiled and put his hand on my shoulder and said, "Thank you for that miracle."

Thomas of Sepphoris

FAMILY SECRETS ARE HARD to keep. I had hoped that mine would not become known to the rest of the disciples. But, like so many things we try to keep hidden, mine came out, and unexpectedly. In my hometown, I am known as Thomas, the Twin. When I was born, I had a twin brother who died when only a few days old. My mother never quite got over it. My Aunt Rachel still says that it was a blessing: "Just think of Jacob and Esau and how they fought and hated each other. Twins can only bring trouble," she would say, and some of the other older women would nod in agreement. I think my mother called me 'the Twin' as a way of remembering, even honoring, my brother. For me, it meant that I often had to explain why I was called by this name. I didn't mind so much as get embarrassed at having to explain. Now, knowing the way the disciples liked to tease each other, here was a fresh target.

Actually, it was Rabbi Yeshua's mother, Mary, who let it be known. Her late husband had relatives in Sepphoris, which is close to Nazareth. She was talking to some family members one day and mentioned that her son had gathered some disciples around him. She named us all and even where we were from. One of her cousins asked if the one named Thomas was also known as 'the Twin.' One night at dinner Mary asked me why I was called 'the Twin,' and so then I had to go through the entire family history in front of everybody. It was embarrassing. Of course, there were the usual jokes that my brother must have been better looking than me. John once said, "I think this explains a lot, because you have enough questions for two people." Then he punched me in the shoulder. I couldn't argue with him because I do ask a lot of questions. Rabbi Yeshua is very patient with me. It seems I need to be certain about some things.

Just a few days ago, we were gathered in a deserted place when crowds of people, I mean, thousands, showed up all of a sudden. They had heard that Rabbi Yeshua was in the area and they came to listen to his stories and preaching, and to receive healings. When the day wore on, we all got nervous because we knew the crowds were getting hungry and there was nothing to feed them. Simon suggested he send them into the nearest town, but Rabbi Yeshua said that we should feed them. Thaddeus blurted out, "With what? We have nothing." Andrew said, "I think my nephew has a lunch," and he retrieved a few loaves of bread and some dried fish. "That's it?" Thaddeus said. "That's all we've got?" Rabbi Yeshua took the bread and fish and told us to have the people sit down and then bring some baskets. We did as he told us, and then he portioned out the food and said a blessing over the baskets. Then he gave them to us and said, "Pass them around to the people." We looked at him with unbelieving eyes, but did as we were told. As the baskets were passed, the people kept pulling out more bread and fish, and more and more, until everyone was fed.

Rabbi Yeshua then asked us to gather up the leftovers. As we did so, I quietly asked Andrew, "How does he do it? I mean, how does he make something out of nothing? I just don't understand." Andrew simply said, "It's a miracle—that's all." "I know", I said, "but I still want to know how he does these things." Andrew laughed and said, "Once you explain a miracle, it is no longer a miracle." Then he added, "Faith, my brother—faith!" We gathered twelve baskets full. As we put them down in front of him, I snuck a piece of bread and ate it just to make sure it was really bread—it was. Rabbi Yeshua saw me do this and asked, "Are you still hungry, or did you just want to make sure it was real? Remember what the Psalmist said, 'Taste and see that the Lord is good; blessed is the one who trusts in Adonai.'" Then he reached into a basket and took a big piece of bread and ate it: "Not as good as my mother's, but good enough." I wanted to ask him for an explanation, but I kept my doubts to myself.

Izaac Ben Eliezar of Jerusalem

THE NEWS FROM GALILEE has been worrisome. There have been more attacks on Romans by the Zealots. Tax collections have been lagging. And then there are more reports about this young Rabbi from Capernaum: strange healings; miracles, if one can believe them; large crowds gathered to hear his sermons. There is even one report he touched a leper and cleansed him—but why touch him and make himself unclean? Why not just cleanse him at a distance and then tell him to go away? Someone told Caiaphas that the leper was in Jerusalem asking to be examined so he could offer the sacrifice for his cleansing. Caiaphas had the Temple Guards find the man. He said to the Sanhedrin, "We need to ask this so-called leper some questions about this Rabbi from Capernaum."

The leper was found in the presence of a Pharisee from Tiberias. Ironically, his name was Eliezar, like my father. The Pharisee was causing a disturbance by cursing the leper and calling him a heretic, claiming that he had been healed by a disciple of Beelzebul and, therefore, his healing was invalid, a sham, and dangerous. I think that some people have a leprosy of the heart. Should we not rejoice that a leper is now clean and can rejoin the people of God? The Temple Guards brought them both to be questioned by the Sanhedrin.

I wonder what my father would have done. He, too, was a Sadducee, from a long line of Temple servants. We disagreed on the need for strong purity and severe separateness. He probably would have encouraged this Galilean prophet, saying we need to be more open to new ideas and less stringent about the Torah, and even about the Temple. He was afraid we would strangle the faith with all of our "Do's and Don'ts." He frowned on the practice of money changers and markets in the Court of the Gentiles. He would often say that even though it was a place for non-Jews, it was still holy ground. We agreed we needed to stay on the good side of the Roman governor and not stir things up, especially at Passover when the crowds were so large. The Romans frown on anything that looks like disorder, much less chaos. I think the money-changers and markets are a reliable source of income for the Temple. I also think we should be more forceful in stopping upstart preachers like this Galilean. They can only bring problems and we can't afford any challenges to the current system of cooperation with the Romans and, I might add, the Pharisees. We need them both to maintain law and order in the country.

When my father became ill a few years ago, he would tell me stories of some of the interesting people he had met over a long career in Jerusalem. He told me once of meeting a young man from Nazareth in Galilee. He had forgotten his name. This young man was around twelve years old and somehow made his way into the Temple during one of the many discussions the Sadducees and Scribes were having on the Torah. He mostly listened, but several times actually joined in and was incredibly bright and insightful. After the discussion, as it was getting late in the day, my father realized that this young man was by himself. He did not know where his parents were, so invited him to stay at our home. I was very young at the time and do not remember this incident. My father spoke of how well this young man understood the Torah and especially the prophets—Isaiah in particular. He had a particular concern for the poor and the weak and the hungry. My father often wondered what happened to him and if he ever became a rabbi or village leader. I wonder if there is a connection between this young man and this Yeshua of Capernaum. I doubt it, but still wonder.

The Sanhedrin gathered in the Temple in the early afternoon. We asked to hear from the Pharisee Eliezar of Tiberias. He entered and bowed to the group. We were all seated while he stood in the center. Caiaphas asked him to tell what he knew of the Rabbi Yeshua from Capernaum. Eliezar became agitated and spat out, "He is a heretic! A son of Beelzebul! He thinks he is above the Torah. He profanes the Sabbath by healing and walking too far from his home. He heals, but by the power of Beelzebul—he is possessed! We saw him heal a lame man, but before doing that he said to the man, 'Your sins are forgiven.' He thinks he is Adonai and has the power to forgive sins. On another occasion, he is said to have healed a leper by touching him. Can you imagine—he touched a leper—clearly against our teachings. He has gathered disciples who are a threat to our people. He has no shame—he speaks openly with women and Gentiles. He even has been seen eating with tax collectors and prostitutes. He thinks he is so clever saying, 'The healthy have no need of a physician. I have come for the sick.' He is a menace to our purity and our way of life.'"

I watched as Caiaphas stroked his chin and asked, "What do you think we should do?" Eliezar quickly replied, "He must be removed, arrested, and, . . ." he hesitated, then said, "destroyed!" After a pause, he continued: "I have spoken to others and they agree. I even went up to Caesarea Philippi and spoke with the Herodians. When I told them of the threat to law and order, they, too, agreed that this Rabbi Yeshua must be stopped." Caiaphas looked around the circle and frowned. He said to the Pharisee, "If what you have said is true, then he is indeed a threat to us and to the whole of the tribes of Israel. But we need more proof, more information. We need to find one of his disciples who will be persuaded to tell us about his teachings and his associations." We all nodded in agreement. Eliezar then said, "If I may be so bold, I think I can befriend some of his disciples and pretend to be a follower and discover which one of those close to him could be turned to our cause." Caiaphas nodded and said, "Good! We send you with our blessing." He stood up and said, "Now, what about that leper?" Zedekiah spoke up and said, "I have examined him and he is clean. He has paid the cost of the sacrifices and is waiting on our ruling." Caiaphas smiled and said, "As long as he has paid—pronounce him clean. And tell him to keep his mouth shut." I walked out of the Temple and took Eliezar by the arm. I wanted to learn more about this Rabbi from Galilee.

Shalomie of Nazareth

JERUSALEM! AT LAST! I couldn't believe that I was really going to go up to Jerusalem. I was, of course, excited. And I was nervous. And I was even a little frightened because there have been threats against Rabbi Yeshua and the other men—the disciples. The first time they all went to Jerusalem, none of the women went with them. Last year at Passover, Mary, Rabbi's mother, was ill, so he asked me to stay with her. But this year, we are all going together. We are leaving soon and expect to get to the city a whole week before the festival. We are already getting together the supplies we will need for the trip. The men are busy drying fish and repairing sandals and baggage packs. The women are baking extra unleavened bread and cleaning skins for water. My cousin, the butcher, is giving us some dried meat to take—not my favorite, but it will be needed. Naturally, the women are making sure we have enough of everything for the trip. A new follower, Mary of Magdala, has asked to come with us. She volunteered to provide two donkeys to help carry the baggage, so we accepted her offer. None of us know her very well, but she is welcome, as Rabbi Yeshua always reminds us. I can't believe it—Passover in Jerusalem! It is a dream come true.

I hope everything goes well. I hope Rabbi Yeshua does not cause another argument with the Pharisees. I admire him very much, but sometimes he can be very provocative, to say the least. Last year at Passover, he healed a blind man—not just any blind man, but one who had been blind from birth. Andrew loves to tell the story. They were all walking in Jerusalem and they met this blind man begging. John asked, "Rabbi, who sinned? This man, or his parents, that he was born blind?" Rabbi surprised everyone when he said, "Neither. This man was born blind not to show punishment, but in order to show the glory and power of God." Then he spat on the ground and made some mud. While he was doing this, he said to the disciples, and I am sure to the surrounding crowd, "While we are here in this world, we must do the things that will reveal God's glory and light. I bring that light into this world because Adonai has sent me to be light in the darkness." Then he rubbed the mud on the blind man's eyes and said, "Go and wash in the pool of Siloam." Andrew and Nathaniel led the man away to the pool.

Later in the day, Rabbi and the disciples met the blind man again, and he told them an amazing story. He had done as Yeshua told him. He went and washed in the pool of Siloam. And he was able to see for the first time in his life. Well, of course, he was excited and began to tell everyone around him he had been born blind and was now healed thanks to a Rabbi from Galilee. The people knew him as a blind beggar, so they took the man to the Pharisees. Andrew and Nathaniel followed along. He told the same story—how Rabbi Yeshua from Galilee had made mud and put it on his eyes, how he then washed in Siloam, and now he could see. Since it was the Sabbath, the Pharisees were very upset that the rules had been broken. They told the man that he was a sinner and asked him to bring his parents. When the parents arrived, they asked, "Is this your son who claims to have been born blind? We don't believe him, and in any case, he has broken the Sabbath rules." The man's parents were overjoyed and embraced their son, but they were afraid of the Pharisees. The father said, "Yes. This is our son. And he was indeed born blind. And we believe his story." The Pharisees said, "Well, we don't believe him. We think you are making this all up. Tell us again what happened." The man born blind said, "Why? Do you want to become his followers, too?" The Pharisees really got mad then and said, "You are all sinners and so is the man who claims to have healed you—he does not obey the Sabbath." The man said, "If he is such a sinner, then why has God listened to him and given him the power to heal blindness?" The Pharisees shouted at the man and his parents, "You are hereby forbidden from entering the Synagogue or the Temple. You are no longer welcome!"

One day I asked Rabbi Yeshua about this incident and he sighed and said that it was true and he looked very sad. He told me he had met the parents and their son later in the day, and they had told him all that had happened. He then said, "I asked them if they believed Adonai will send the Son of Man to bring judgment into the world. I told them I have come to bring both judgment and light, so that the blind can see and those who think they see will be blind. The Pharisees are blind guides; they think they see, but they do not. They are too sure of themselves, too proud, too self-righteous.

Therefore, their sin remains." I must have looked frightened because he looked at me and smiled: "I did not mean to scare you. But you need to understand that what we are doing is truly a matter of life and death." I tried not to show it, but his words worried me. As excited as I was to go up to Jerusalem, I suddenly had a dark premonition that there would be trouble.

Hannah of Jericho

I NEVER THOUGHT I would see the day when Zacchaeus got joy out of being generous. But it happened. In fact, it is still happening. I have lived in Jericho for most of my life. For many years now I have been the cook in the house of Zacchaeus, the chief tax collector in this area of Palestine. He is probably the most hated and feared man in Jericho because he controls how much everyone has to pay in taxes. He also controls the passage of caravans and traders on the route through the Jordan Valley and the road up to Jerusalem. Needless to say, he is rich—very rich. Zacchaeus himself is kind of short. But when he comes to collect your taxes, he always brings along a few very tall, muscular men. Sometimes he even has Roman soldiers accompany him. So, who would not pay up what he demands? To keep on the good side of the Romans, he even changed his name to sound more Roman, Zacchaeus instead of Zakkai. It is ironic, even blasphemous, since his name in Aramaic means "righteous one"—and believe me, he is far from righteous. He will do almost anything to keep the favor of the Romans. Like my father used to say, "It's not what you know, but who you know—and that is NOT in the Torah."

At any rate, I try to keep his household and workers well fed and happy. Zacchaeus especially likes my mujadrah and lamb stew. He enjoys eating most everything I cook, but I have to remind him of the Jewish dietary restrictions. He is usually understanding, but sometimes gets annoyed with the limitations. Well, about a week ago, I was at the market to buy some things—and also to gossip—when I heard that this popular Rabbi from Capernaum was coming down the Jordan Valley on his way to Jerusalem for Passover. We had all heard about him and how he was "causing trouble and turning things upside down!" At least that is what my friend Miriam was saying. She was arguing with another farmer's wife who supported Rabbi Yeshua and his concern for the poor and his criticism of the Pharisees: "Look how he heals everyone! Look at how he treats women! Look at how he rebukes the rich—he sounds like Amos!" Miriam shouted back, "And just like Amos, he is causing trouble. No good will come of this. He will end up in a Roman prison—or worse!" I asked, "When is he coming to Jericho? And I need some lentils and some of those fresh greens." Miriam said, "He is supposed to arrive tomorrow. Sounds like there will be a parade. Just what we need. How much lentils?" I said, "Enough for ten people. And some wheat and barley. I love parades. I think I will come and watch." Miriam snorted, and with an annoyed look, filled my sacks. "Why don't you bring old Zacchaeus with you? Maybe the Rabbi can heal him of being a thief and robber. Only he is so short the Rabbi probably wouldn't even notice him." I smiled and said, "Now don't make fun of the man just because he is small." I thanked her as I left the market. Miriam shouted after me, "Small minded is more like it! And a traitor!"

The next morning, I mentioned to Zacchaeus that there was going to be a parade in Jericho because a young Rabbi from Capernaum was coming through town. "He has caused a stir among the people and especially the Pharisees. People say he has great powers and heals many of their disease and illness. They say he even healed a man born blind." Zacchaeus thought for a moment and then said, "I think I will stay at home and look over my accounts this morning. I don't seem to get on well with rabbis. But, thanks for letting me know." I finished up in the kitchen and walked toward Jericho with two other servants. By the time we got to the main road, there was already a crowd gathered. I saw Thalia and her husband, a farmer, and asked them for any news. She told me that Rabbi Yeshua was very near Jericho. He had stopped to heal a blind beggar who is now walking with him and his disciples. Some people are upset that he is walking together with several women, who are also his disciples.

The crowd increased in the next few minutes, so there was a line of people on either side of the road. A young man suddenly came running down the road shouting, "He is coming! He is coming!" We all craned our necks to look north on the road, and we could see a group of about twenty people walking toward us. Soon they were very close and people were calling out to the young Rabbi, asking for healing and a blessing. Someone hollered, "Go back to Capernaum!" and was quickly shouted down. When Rabbi Yeshua was almost next to us, he stopped and looked over our heads. He came up to Thalia's husband and asked, "Who is the man in the tree?" Suddenly we all turned and looked and, I couldn't believe my eyes, there was Zacchaeus, halfway up a sycamore tree. Several men laughed, and then one said, "Oh, that is Zacchaeus, our chief tax collector." Another man said, "I wish he would stay up in the tree." Rabbi Yeshua parted the crowd and came to the base of the tree and said, "Zacchaeus! Come down! I have to stay at your house today." We were all amazed. I guess he did not know what kind of man Zacchaeus was, or how hated he was by the people of Jericho. One bystander grumbled, "Rabbi, this man is a thief and a sinner. He steals from us all and has gotten rich from our taxes." Rabbi Yeshua smiled and said, "Then he needs me more than anyone else."

Zacchaeus scrambled down the tree and brushed himself off, trying to look dignified. He said, "Rabbi, you are welcome at my home. And all of your disciples as well." He looked over at me and said, "Hannah! Go to the market and get enough for everyone—the best. We are going to have guests for dinner." I quickly found the two other servants, and we returned to the market. I told them what we would need and that I would have to go to the butcher for some lamb. I was very nervous because I had never cooked for so many people before. By the time we got back to Zacchaeus' house, some disciples were resting under the trees while two of the men were playing with his children. We went into the kitchen to prepare the meal when several women disciples came in to help and two young men asked if they needed water from the well.

After several hours of cooking, the meal was a great success. While we were cleaning up the dishes and pots, one of the young servants was telling us what she had overheard while pouring wine and bringing water so everyone could wash their hands and feet. Zacchaeus was trying to explain to Rabbi Yeshua how he kept his religion and his business separate, as if he had two separate boxes. Rabbi Yeshua said that was like having two masters and that is dangerous because you will love one and hate the other. Then he told a story about the steward of a wealthy man who went on a journey and put the steward in charge. The steward both cheated his master and defrauded some customers. When the rich man returned, he heard of the steward's behavior and told him to get his accounts in order because he would be fired. The steward was too proud to beg and too out of shape to do manual labor. Instead, he called in some of his master's debtors and told them to pay only a portion of their debt while he marked it paid in full. When the master heard of this, he commended the steward for being so shrewd. Zacchaeus interrupted and said that was fraudulent and unethical. Rabbi Yeshua nodded and said it was true. Then he said, "You cannot have two masters. You cannot serve God and money." Zacchaeus was silent and then said, "I think I get it. I think I must choose one or the other." "What will you do?" asked the Rabbi. "I don't know," said the little man, as he stood up and walked into his garden.

While I was finishing up the pots and putting away the dishes, Rabbi Yeshua and his disciples came into the kitchen to thank us for the wonderful meal. They were preparing to leave when Zacchaeus burst into the room and said, "I have decided what to do. Call the leaders of the community together. Invite them to my home for an announcement." We were all very surprised and puzzled. He sent two young men into Jericho to call the elders together. We waited in the garden until they were all assembled. Zacchaeus then stood up and said, "I will give away half of my wealth to assist the poor. Also, if I have defrauded anyone, I will repay them four times over." No one said a word. We were all stunned. Finally, Rabbi Yeshua laughed, came forward, embraced Zacchaeus, and said, "Today salvation has come to this house. Here is a true child of Abraham. For the Son of Man has come to seek out and save the lost." During the hubbub that followed, I found Rabbi Yeshua and said to him: "Thank you for giving people a second chance." He whispered to me, "Sometimes I think my main job in life is giving people second chances." A cheer went up from all the elders. I couldn't wait to tell Miriam.

Josiah of Bethphage

MY OLDER BROTHER AND I were throwing stones down the slope from the Mount of Olives. I know we are not supposed to do this, but it so much fun to watch the stones bounce off of the boulders and skip down into the valley below. We are always careful not to throw when there are people on the paths heading for Jerusalem. I think the Mount of Olives is the best place in the world to see the city. Sometimes we play we are soldiers in the army of King David and we march around looking for Philistines. King David must have had a magnificent palace where the Temple is now. I often imagine what it must have looked like before King Solomon built the first Temple. I don't think the walls were as high as they are now, but I am sure it was even more beautiful, and bright white with lots of caravans from faraway places coming to pay tribute to the king. Our grandfather always reminds us that Jerusalem must always be respected and that we must always obey the Torah, "Or else!" One of grandfather's favorite expressions was "Or else!" He would say things like, "Honor the Sabbath, or else . . ." And "Obey your parents, or else!" He then would tell us the tragic story of the destruction of Jerusalem by the Babylonians, all because the people disobeyed Adonai. He would then move into his warnings about being ready for the Messiah: "And when Messiah comes, he will be seen first on the Mount of Olives— just like Zechariah said—and the mountain will be split in two, and a rush of water shall come from Jerusalem, fill the land, and all the people will come to worship Adonai, and then Messiah will enter Jerusalem and will reign forever." Then he would pause and look hard at us and say, "So we must always be ready, or else!"

Last week we had a strange thing happen. It was late in the morning and two men came down the road from Bethany, a short distance away. They were strangers. They entered the village and looked around until they found a colt tied to a tree. One of the men asked, "Has this colt ever been ridden?"

Simon's father said, "No. It is still very young." The two men looked at each other and untied the colt. Several of us said, "What are you doing untying that colt?" The men said, "Our Rabbi needs it. We will bring it back after he has ridden into the city." I thought no one would let them just take the colt. They were strangers—why should we trust them? But no one said anything. It was very strange. After they left, my father said to me, "Follow them and keep an eye out to make sure they remember to bring the colt back here. You are small and no one will notice that you are following them."

I followed them back to Bethany, to the home of Mary and Martha and Lazarus, whom we know. There were about twenty people waiting. They were all thrilled to see the colt. A very tall man threw a cloak over the colt's back. Another of the men, I think he was the Rabbi, got on the colt. The young animal was frightened at first. The Rabbi was able to calm him down. They all set off on the road that goes down the Mount of Olives, across the Kidron Valley and into Jerusalem through the gate at the Temple. The road was already crowded with pilgrims coming to Jerusalem for the Passover, so it was sometimes difficult to keep track of the colt. The crowd around the Rabbi was getting larger and people were singing Psalms. Then a few people threw cloaks on the path in front of the Rabbi shouting, "Hosanna! Blessed is the one who comes in the name of Adonai!" Then there were more cheers. Someone near me asked another, "Who is this man on the colt?" The other replied, "He is the prophet, the Rabbi from Nazareth." Some people even cut off tree branches and threw them in his path. I did not understand what was happening.

The crowd was getting thicker, and I was afraid I would lose the colt, so I pushed ahead until I was almost next to it. People were yelling back and forth to each other, telling how this Rabbi had healed a blind man and a leper and a little girl who was thought to be dead. One woman cried out, "Maybe he is the Messiah." Another one said, "All I know is that he speaks for Adonai. He speaks the truth." As we got near to the city, some Pharisees blocked the road and said, "Rabbi, tell your disciples to be quiet!" The Rabbi laughed and said, "Even if they were quiet, all these stones would cry out." When they tried to stop him, the crowd got louder and pushed through shouting, "Hosanna! Hosanna to the one who is coming." It almost made me want to shout too.

The crowd pushed and squeezed to get through the gate. There were some Roman soldiers standing near the gate, and they looked very nervous. Once we all got inside, the Rabbi dismounted and one of his followers took the colt's rope and led him to one side. I realized he wanted to follow the Rabbi, so I saw my chance and asked him if he wanted me to guard the colt until they were ready to leave the city. He gave me the rope and said he would pay me when he came back, "Soon. I hope." I took the rope as he ran off. I looked for some grass, but there was none. Then I remembered the tree branches that people had thrown in front of the Rabbi. I tied the colt to a column and went to find some branches. When I came back, there was an old man looking at the colt—I think he was praying. I offered the branches to the colt, which chewed on them gratefully. The old man came up and stroked the colt's back. "Is this the colt that the Rabbi from Nazareth rode today?" I said, "Yes. Why?" He said, "Do you know Zechariah?" I replied, "You mean the prophecy about the Mount of Olives?" "Yes!" he said, "And also how the king will come into Jerusalem humbly, riding on a colt, not a war horse—and how this king will not proclaim war but peace, peace in all the world. Do you know this?" I said nothing. I was afraid.

Just then some people came running from the direction of the Temple. Then more and more people came running and talking loudly. The Roman soldiers at the gate grabbed a man and asked what was going on. The man said, "There is some wild man in the Court of the Gentiles—overturning the tables of the moneychangers and chasing the merchants away, calling them a den of thieves. He released some doves from their cages and set free all the goats and lambs. He's crazy." The captain of the soldiers left two at the gate and ran toward the Temple with the others, pushing against the crowd. The old man went back to his praying, and I kept feeding the colt.

About an hour later, two of the followers of the Rabbi came and said they had to return the colt to the village on the Mount of Olives. We walked back through the gate and began up the road to Bethphage. One man picked me up and put me on the colt: "Here! You may as well ride. It's a steep road. You can pretend you are a king." I was silent for a while then asked, "What happened at the Temple?" They both laughed and shook their heads. "I wish he would have told us what he was going to do," said the one. "Does he ever tell us," said the other. "He could have gotten us arrested or even killed with his 'righteous anger' Those Romans were in no mood for 'righteous anger' of any kind—especially from Jews. They were ready to arrest someone." Then, turning to me, he said, "I feel Rabbi Yeshua did not like the presence of the moneychangers or the merchants or the animals for sale. I agree they are all a bunch of crooks, but they have been doing this for years." The other man said, "His point was, as he said, 'My house shall be a called a house of prayer; and you have made it a den of thieves.' He got that right!" I thought for a moment and then remembered my grandfather, and said, "So maybe he is getting the Temple prepared for the coming of the Messiah. I mean, this is the Mount of Olives, so anything could happen." The two men stopped walking and looked at me with surprise. "I hope you are right," said the one. The other shook his head: "Rabbi will need a lot more help than his aging mother and a rag-tag bunch of men and women from Galilee and wherever. If he is the Messiah, he will need to call on all the angels from heaven to win this fight." I quietly imagined the clouds opening and the hosts of Adonai rushing down to defeat the Romans. I thought to myself that I would have to keep an eye on this Rabbi, or else!

Eleazar Scribe of Jerusalem

ACTUALLY, I AM SURPRISED that it did not happen long before this. To-day my son Izaak came home from the Temple and told me that a young Rabbi from Galilee had entered the Temple, the Court of the Gentiles, and shouted at the money changers and those selling sacrificial animals. He then turned over some of their tables and declared, "It is written 'My house shall be a house of prayer;' but you have made it a den of thieves." He then smashed some cages, releasing the doves, and chased some of the other animals into the crowd. He made a cord of rope into a whip and threatened some sellers and money changers. I guess by the time the Temple guards arrived, he and his disciples had created a major melee. Izaak said that some of the poor in the crowd cheered him on, while the Temple workers were scandalized. They should be scandalized by the prices they charge and the way they cheat the people wanting to buy just a few doves, not to mention a lamb. He said that they never caught up with him because the crowd was all in his favor and blocked the guards from getting close enough to arrest him. I wish I had been there—one drawback of getting old.

I come from a family of Jerusalem Scribes. We have been working in the Temple for a long, long time. I have had to stop my service because of ill health. My son, Izaak, now takes my place. He keeps me up to date on the latest intrigues and actions of the Sanhedrin, and the gossip. Neither of us are supporters of Caiaphas, the high priest, nor of Annas, his father-in-law. Somehow, they have been able to pass this position back and forth for many years, thanks to their alliance with Pilate and the Romans. They are the ones responsible for the outrage of the young Rabbi today. They have become greedy and have raised the prices on sacrificial animals and the exchange rates. Many who come to make sacrifice bring only Roman or Greek money and so have to exchange it for Temple currency that is "pure," as if our Jewish money is any cleaner that the other. And the simple, pious folks just want to follow the Torah and make the required sacrifice. So, they are stuck, and are taken advantage of. I am glad someone has finally stood up to these inequities. I would like to meet this young Rabbi from Galilee.

Izaak says that there are darker things going on in the inner circle at the Temple. Annas and Caiaphas have made common cause with the Pharisees, and even brought in some of the Herodians, of all people. Apparently, they are all trying to figure out a way to get rid of this young man, this Rabbi from Galilee. I think someone said he was from Capernaum, or was it Nazareth—whatever! He seems to be very popular with the crowds of poor people, so they are afraid to even try to arrest him. Izaak heard from one of the guards that this young Rabbi was rather brazen this morning. He came to Jerusalem from the Mount of Olives, which is the traditional place where the Messiah will come from. And he went even further, entering the city riding on a colt, an obvious reference to Zechariah's prophecy: "Behold, your king comes to you; triumphant and victorious, humble and riding on a colt." And the crowds, apparently, figured it out and threw cloaks and palm branches in his path; and then they began to chant, "Hosanna! Hosanna to the son of David—the one who comes in the name of Adonai!" When they came to the city gate, one priest shouted, "Tell your disciples to be quiet and stop shouting." Well, the young Rabbi looked up and said, "Why? If they are silent, even the stones would cry out." I doubt that went over very well with the priests.

After he entered the city, he went to the Temple and caused quite a scene. Izaak said he was curious to find out more about this young man, so he agreed to join a group of Scribes who went out looking for him. They had planned to question him. When they eventually found him, surrounded by his disciples and a large crowd of people, they said, "We want to ask you a question." He said, "Certainly. Ask whatever you want." The Scribes asked him, "We know what you did this morning at the Temple, and we want to ask you by what authority you did those things?" The young Rabbi stood up and said, "First, let me ask you a question: the baptism of John, was it from heaven or of human origin?" Izaak said he was impressed with the question. The Scribes talked among themselves and said, "If we say it was from heaven then he will ask us why we did not accept it. If we say it was merely of human origin, then the crowd will get angry because they honor John as a prophet." Izaak smiled and then said, "So they told him, 'We do not know.'" The young Rabbi got angry and said, "Then neither will I tell you by what authority I do these things." Izaak then frowned and said he was worried because as they were leaving, he heard the Rabbi tell the crowds: "Beware of the Scribes, blind guides, hypocrites. They tithe mint and dill and cumin, but they neglect the weightier matters of the Torah—justice, and mercy, and faith." He said he wanted to stay and hear more from the young Rabbi, but he was afraid the other Scribes would not understand and think of him as a sympathizer, which would, of course, have been true.

As I reflected on these strange happenings, I began to reminisce and was reminded of another strange occurrence many years ago—maybe 30 years ago. I was a young Scribe in Jerusalem and happened upon a young boy from Galilee. He was by himself in the Temple. It was during the days of Passover. He was listening to the debates and discussions of the Priests and Scribes. I remember being amazed when he began asking them questions and giving his understandings of Torah, which were wise beyond his years. I also remember that he had been left behind by his parents—purely a misunderstanding—and that I took him home with me and kept him with me until his parents came for him the next day. His father was furious, and rightfully so. I remember, also, that he told me he wanted to be a rabbi. I wonder—could it be? I wonder if he is the same young man. Probably not—even so, I wonder.

Annas the Priest of Jerusalem

WHAT'S NEXT? THE END of the World? The Day of the Lord? Maybe Amos was right. I feel like I have run from a lion only to meet up with a bear. Or I've entered a house to hide and put my hand on a wall, only to be bitten by a snake. With everything else that threatens us, now we have a self-styled 'Messiah' causing a riot at the Temple. And he is not even from Bethlehem, but from Galilee, of all backward places. I have heard of him before, but I didn't think he would be so brazen to take his claim to the Temple—and right before Passover. It all makes me nervous. And worse, it will make the Romans nervous.

First it was the cult at Qumran attacking the Temple with their so-called "Teacher of Righteousness." They claimed they were the only ones fit to serve in the Temple. They even compiled a list of all those who were worthy to serve as high priest and claimed we were usurpers and illegitimate. They also called us corrupt and impure. I thought we were rid of them when Herod silenced that John the Baptizer recently. I wonder if this new "Messiah" has any connections to Qumran. Probably not since he talks about mercy and not so much about purity. Maybe he just wants to be high priest instead of Caiaphas.

And then there are the Zealots who want to be like the Maccabees and set up a real kingdom. They are a thorn in the side of the Romans. Maybe they are more a sword in the side of the Romans since they send out these assassins—these sicarii—to eliminate Roman leaders, and even some Jewish collaborators. They are a distraction, but as long as they stay in the north and the hill country, the Romans can take care of them. In fact, they have one in prison right now—his name is Barabbas—a thief and a murderer. He is due to be crucified this week, I believe.

The Romans have taken from us the threat of the death penalty. We could do a lot more to silence some of these trouble makers even if we did not use it very often. I think back on Alexander Jannaeus. He may have over-done it when he crucified those 800 Pharisees at the Feast of Tabernacles, but at least he kept the peace. Speaking of the Pharisees, we will need them on our side if we are to deal with this new "Messiah" from Galilee. They have more influence in that part of Israel, and they are already upset that he has become so popular with the crowds and the poor. They have been talking to the Scribes and Elders here in Jerusalem, and they think they have convinced one of his disciples to tell us his plans and even help hand him over to us before Passover—anything to keep the Romans happy and in their barracks.

The Romans have been helpful to me over the years. At least they un-derstand the nature of power—you scratch my back and I'll scratch yours. In fact, I owe my career to a Roman, Quirinius, who was governor of Syria many years ago. Through him, I was able to remain the high priest for many years. I had five sons, and several of them also have been high priest. My third son, Joseph Caiaphas, is now the high priest. I still keep my hand in things and advise him about how to handle some of the issues that come up. I urge him every day to make sure that he keeps the Romans happy, which means that he must keep the people of Jerusalem calm and settled. This is especially im-portant during the feast days when there are so many more coming in from the countryside and the hill country, from Galilee and the Negev, as well as Egypt and Syria. I advised him to double the Temple guards and to make sure that there were no disturbances like the one this morning. This is important also because during the feast days we make a lot more income from sacrifices and offerings. How else are we to maintain our way of life and our wealth?

I have called Caiaphas to come to my quarters today so we can plan what to do about this so-called "Messiah" from Galilee. I will counsel him to remember that it is better that one man die than have the entire nation destroyed. We will have to devise a strategy to arrest him when he is alone or away from the crowds. It will be easy to find someone who, for a few denarii, will give testimony against him. Blasphemy seems to be the best charge, but we will also have to charge him with treason against the Em-peror to get him executed. I will have to speak with Pilate when he arrives from Caesarea. We will need him to support our plan. He can sometimes be difficult to deal with. He just doesn't give a damn about our ways, our religious rules. He might want to release this Rabbi Yeshua just to spite us. We will have to stir up the people against this pretender. We have little time with Passover coming at the end of the week. We must deal with this annoyance in order to have a peaceful, holy Passover.

Rahab of Jerusalem

It was the last thing that I had that was worth anything. Everything else had been taken from me. This one gift I wanted to give away on my own. I had lost everything. I had lost my husband. I had lost my two children. I had even lost my house. And, worst of all, I had lost my dignity and piety. Only a few years ago, my life had been wonderful and joyous. I was married to a wonderful man who loved me. We had two sons who were a lot to deal with, but I loved being a mother. We lived in a nice house near Jerusalem. My husband traveled a lot buying spices, and oils, and perfumes which he sold in the city. When he returned from one trip, he gave me a precious gift: an alabaster jar filled with nard. He said, "Guard this carefully; it is worth many denarii." I was amazed and wrapped it in a shawl and placed it in a basket in our bedroom. From time to time, I would open it and walk around the room so that the aroma could fill the house. Then, after a long trip away, he came home with a fever and became very ill. After a few days, the two boys also became ill, and both died quickly. Then my husband died too. I was now a widow and childless. Our friends and neighbors were kind, but I was crushed.

A few weeks after their deaths, my late husband's trading partner came to the house and asked if he could use our house to meet with some merchants. I did not want to seem unfriendly, so I agreed. As he was leaving, he made several comments that I was still a very beautiful young woman, and that I should consider re-marrying. I am sure he was trying to flatter me, but I was not interested. A few days later he returned with two merchants and some baskets of food, which he asked me to prepare for their evening meal. I agreed. They also had brought some jugs of wine and began to drink as they discussed plans for their next trip. After the dinner was served and cleaned up, I thought they would leave, but they continued to drink. Soon they demanded that I dance for them. I refused and went into my bedroom and closed the door. I heard them laughing and singing. I became frightened. Suddenly, the door burst open and the two merchants came into my room and pushed me onto the bed. Then they raped me—they raped me in my own home. I cried out, but they muffled my voice and threatened to hurt me. I was terrified.

When they were finished, they both left and talked quietly with my husband's partner. He came into the bedroom and I was prepared to be raped again. But he sat on the side of the bed and said that if I told anyone, he would spread the word to the community that I had become a prostitute in order to make money to keep my house. He stroked my head and even kissed me and said, "I will help you. You should be very nice to me." Then he left. I did not know what to do. I was afraid to tell anyone. So, I kept quiet. I did not even tell my sister-in-law or my best friend next door. I washed myself three times each day, but it did not help. A few days later, my husband's partner returned and offered to marry me and to buy my house. I told him to leave and never return. Soon I realized that my neighbors were avoiding me and the shopkeepers were gruff with me. At the market, I was often ignored by the sellers, and when I asked for fruits and vegetables, they were curt and sharp with me. I knew what had happened. My reputation had been destroyed by my late husband's partner. The next time he came, I agreed to sell him the house. But I would not marry him. I would rather die—and almost did.

I found a small house in a nearby village. But the money soon ran out, and I was forced to beg. I was offered money for sex and finally fell into the practice of prostitution. In public, I was shunned—until some man needed my services. The Pharisees were the worst. They shouted at me and threatened to stone me. I became hardened to everyone. I was still beautiful, so I was desired by many. But inside I felt hollow, empty, and dull. Then, one evening, I met a man who smiled at me in a kind and gentle way. At first, I thought he just wanted what other men wanted. But he asked me my name and invited me to dinner with him and his friends. I was wary, but I accepted. When I came to dinner, he introduced me to his friends and asked me to sit at the table. I looked around and saw about a dozen young men, and then I noticed two other prostitutes and even a tax collector. I was amazed. I suddenly felt like a human being again. He spoke kindly to everyone and told some wonderful stories and parables about love and mercy and forgiveness. I asked one of the young men who he was, and he replied he was Rabbi Yeshua from Capernaum. And more than that, he was the

Messiah of Adonai, the bringer of good news to the poor and outcast, to all who need healing and comfort.

That night I had a dream that he would soon die. He would be killed by those who feared his message of mercy and peace and love for all people, regardless of their place in society. I saw he would be killed by the powerful and that it would happen soon. I was then determined to offer my gift to him—a gift for his burial. In the morning I went looking for him, but was told that he was in Bethany with friends. I returned to my house and uncovered the alabaster jar with the nard. I opened it one last time and let the aroma waft through the room. Then I closed the lid and wrapped it in my shawl. I made my way out of Jerusalem, up the path to the Mount of Olives, and on to Bethany. By the time I got there, it was late. I asked for the Rabbi from Galilee and was told that he was at dinner in the home of Simon the leper. I found the house and slipped quietly into the kitchen. Then I followed one server into the dining area and came up behind Rabbi Yeshua. I had picked up a stone on my way in order to break the jar. I lifted the alabaster jar and cracked it open and poured the nard over his head. Needless to say, everyone, especially Rabbi Yeshua, was surprised. He turned and looked at me and smiled: "Thank you," he said.

At once the recriminations began: "Who let this woman in the door?" "We all know what kind of woman she is." "How can he allow her to even touch him?" "Why was this ointment wasted? It could have been sold for over three hundred denarii and the money given to the poor?" "Throw her out!" Rabbi Yeshua then stood up and said, "Leave her alone; why do you trouble her?" He took my hand and said, "She has done a beautiful thing for me. The poor you will always have with you, and you can show kindness to them whenever you wish. But you will not always have me with you. She has anointed my body beforehand for my burial." I began to weep when he spoke of his death. He continued to hold my hand and said to those gathered, "Truly, truly I tell you all, wherever the good news of Adonai is proclaimed, even throughout the whole world, what she has done this night will be told and re-told in remembrance of her." The entire room was silent as I turned and walked out past the guests and Simon and the servants. I walked out into the night, down the rocky path, back to Jerusalem, back to my poor house, into my room, and onto my knees—able to pray for the first time in months.

Shalomie of Nazareth

HERE WE ARE IN Jerusalem. Two widows. Doing what we have been doing for years and years—preparing a meal. Though I am not sure what kind of meal it is. We thought it would be a Passover meal. But Passover is not until tomorrow. We have all gathered here because Rabbi Yeshua asked us to be here with him. Several of the disciples found this room on the upper floor of a large house. The kitchen, naturally, is on the lower floor so we will do a lot of steps today. That's all right. I am here with my oldest friend, Mary, Rabbi's mother. We were both young mothers in Nazareth and shared most of our family life with each other. I was heartbroken when she moved to Capernaum three years ago, yet we kept in touch and when my husband died, I, too, moved to Capernaum. I was quickly swept up into the work of her son and his disciples. I suppose I am one of them now. I marvel at his powers of healing and the hope he brings to so many of the poor and troubled of our land. I worry, though, that he has gone too far in his outspoken criticism of the Temple and the Scribes and Pharisees. Today, especially, he seems to be preoccupied and talks about this being his last time in Jerusalem and how he wants to be together with us one more time.

Mary won't talk about her fears and tries to focus on the supper we are to prepare. Twice, now, I have caught her in tears—she blames the onions. I asked Mary of Magdala and she just shakes her head and says that we must make tonight a special night. Our friend Joanna comes and goes since she is the one who is paying for all the food and bread and wine. She, too, is worried and says that she has heard disturbing rumors among both the priests and the Romans. She won't tell exactly what is being said, only that it is troubling. So, we go on with our preparation of the lamb and the vegetables and the bread and the fruit. Joanna has been very generous. I must say a special thank you to her when I see her. The mother of James and John is also with us, and a few other women who came with us from Galilee. With all twelve disciples and us women, it will be a crowded upper room tonight. Rabbi Yeshua has asked for a large pitcher of water and some towels. He would not say why they are needed, only that they will be important. Then he smiled and said, "And lots of bread and wine." His smile faded quickly, and I was again worried about what was going to happen to him.

We finished the preparation: the lamb was roasted, the vegetables were cooked, the fruit was cut, and the bread was baked. Rabbi Yeshua asked us all to come to the room upstairs where he had us sit at several large tables. He told us we needed to be cleaner before Adonai, and so he would wash our feet. We were all surprised, even shocked. I had never had my feet washed by a rabbi, much less by a man. He started with his mother, who immediately began to weep. He then moved to several other women and at last to me. He removed my sandals and held my feet tenderly in his hands. He looked up at me and whispered, "Your feet are tired. They have traveled many miles." I smiled through my tears as he washed my feet and then wiped them. He moved on to his disciples, who were very uncomfortable with this action. When he came to Simon, that big man said, "You will never wash my feet." Rabbi Yeshua looked calmly at him and said, "If I don't wash your feet, then you will have no part of me." Simon said, "Then wash all of me!" Rabbi Yeshua laughed and said, "Your feet will be enough."

When he had finished, he put his robe back on and sat down. "Do you know what I have done for you? You should all then wash each other's feet. You will be servants of each other, and of all that you meet. There will be no one who is not worthy of your love and care—even to the washing of their feet." He continued, "I have desired to have this meal with you because I will not eat with you again until I eat with you in the Kingdom of Adonai, the Kingdom of peace and new life." We were all silent. Finally, he said, "It is time to eat and rejoice. The women have prepared a wonderful meal for us, so let us bless them and the food which they have prepared." Mary was the first to rise and descend to the kitchen. Thankfully, several of the men came down to carry the heavy plates and jugs of wine up the stairs. We began in silence, but gradually the conversation became livelier.

When the meal was almost finished, Rabbi Yeshua asked for a large cup of wine and a plate of bread, which he put in front of him. Then he said a blessing and took the bread and broke off a piece and gave it to John, who was seated next to him. "Take this and eat it," he said. "This is my body, which is broken for all of you." John took the bread and passed it to Bartholomew, who also took a piece. Rabbi Yeshua then added, "Do this in remembrance of me." So, it was passed around to everyone—in stunned silence. Then Rabbi Yeshua took the cup of wine, lifted it up with a blessing and gave it to John, saying, "Take this and drink. This is my blood, which is shed for all of you. Do this in remembrance of me." So, the cup was passed around to everyone—in stunned silence. I looked at Mary and she looked at me, and we both knew that her son would not live long.

Rabbi Yeshua then took a piece of bread and dipped it into the wine and leaned over to Judas, and gave it to him as he whispered something in his ear. Judas looked surprised and then ate the bread and got up and left. We all thought that he had been given a job to do—only much later would we learn what he was to do. Mary of Magdala was the first to get up and begin clearing the dishes. We all followed her lead and cleared the tables, taking the empty dishes down to the kitchen to be washed. James called out that we should make sure that any leftovers were shared with the poor and any beggars in the streets. When all the dishes were cleared, Rabbi Yeshua came down the stairs and thanked Joanna for her generosity. He then thanked all of us women for the delicious meal and gave his mother a hug. He apologized, but he was going over to the Garden of Gethsemane to pray, and he wanted his disciples with him. Mary said, "Just like all men. Eat and find some excuse to leave." We all laughed as she pushed him out the door: "Go pray! All of you, go pray!" When she turned back to us, she was crying. None of us knew then that she would never touch him again until he was dead.

Josiah of Bethphage

MY COUSIN JETHRO AND I were dropping pebbles down the well in the Garden called Gethsemane. It was a very hot evening, so we had left our nightshirts at home and were only wearing linen loin clothes. His family had come to Jerusalem for Passover and was staying with my family in Bethphage. We had decided after dinner to wait until it was dark and then sneak out to explore whatever there was to find. We had come to the Garden because I knew it would be cool. Suddenly we heard voices and saw the light from a torch. We ducked into the olive grove and climbed an old tree to watch. We saw a group of men coming up the path. I recognized them from several days ago when they borrowed a colt from our village. They took it back to Bethany, and I was sent along to watch over the colt and to make sure they brought it back. They had used it for their leader to ride into Jerusalem, and there had been quite a stir—some say it was a riot—at the Temple. Their leader, some Rabbi named Yeshua, had upset the tables and thrown out the moneychangers, but he left before he could be arrested. All I was worried about was getting the colt back home, which I did.

When I looked again, I recognized him, that Rabbi. He was talking to the others, and then he took three of them and moved deeper into the olive grove. We could hear him tell them to wait and keep watch while he went to pray. I told Jethro to be silent, and we climbed down from the tree. We snuck around to where that Rabbi was sitting on a large rock. He was mumbling something. I couldn't hear exactly what he was saying, but I noticed he was sweating a lot. In fact, in the dark, it looked like he was sweating blood. I believe he was terrified. At one point he looked up at the dark sky and said aloud, "Abba, Father, to you all things are possible, so please, please take this cup from me." Then he bowed his head and a few moments later, looked up again and said, "Not what I want, but what you want." I guessed he was praying, but I did not know what "cup" he was talking about. We looked at each other and shrugged, trying not to laugh.

The Rabbi got back up and went back to the other men, who had fallen asleep. He shook his head and said, "Asleep! You couldn't stay awake for just an hour!" He turned and went back to the rock and prayed some more. We waited and watched until he went back and found them still asleep. He roused them and said, "The spirit is willing, but the flesh is weak. Too much good food and wine. You had better be careful that you don't fall into a deeper sleep and miss what Adonai is doing tonight." The others slowly woke up and none of them said anything. They all looked ashamed. We were about to sneak away when we heard more voices down the path. The Rabbi said, "It is enough! The time has come! The Son of Man is about to be handed over to sinners." Jethro and I quickly climbed back up into the olive tree to watch.

A large group of men carrying torches entered the Garden. There were Temple guards and others with swords and clubs. They blocked the path. One man came forward, then hesitated. We could hear some of the Rabbi's men say, "It's Judas! What is he doing with this crowd?" The one whom we guessed was Judas stepped closer and said, "Rabbi," and then kissed him. The guards jumped forward and laid their hands on Rabbi Yeshua, who shouted, "So, you have come to arrest me with swords and clubs as if I were a bandit. Why didn't you arrest me when I was in the Temple teaching and preaching? Why wait until after dark?" The disciples had come forward to protect Rabbi Yeshua and were pushed back and threatened. One disciple, a tall man, pulled out a sword and swung at those trying to arrest the Rabbi. Someone ducked, but not before the sword struck his head and cut off his ear. Jethro screamed, but luckily no one heard him. The Rabbi turned to the tall man and angrily said, "Put away your sword—if you live by the sword, you will die by the sword." Then he reached down and picked up the severed ear and put it back on the bleeding man's head. The bleeding stopped and the man's ear, believe it or not, was healed. Jethro and I looked at each other in disbelief.

All at once, all the Rabbi's followers ran away into the night. One guard yelled, "Let them go! We have our man! Now we will take him to the high priest!" The crowd turned to go back to Jerusalem. The only one left standing in the middle of the Garden was the one they called Judas. Jethro said, "I think he is crying. We better go, too." We climbed down the tree and Jethro started back toward Bethpage, but I was still curious. I told him, "Go on back. And be quiet! Don't make any noise when you crawl in the window." He left, and I followed the crowd. I must have gotten too close because one man saw me and yelled, "Well, look at this! Another disciple!" He chased me and grabbed at my loin cloth. Luckily it ripped away, and I managed to get away—naked—but free. I ran all the way home, praying that I did not run into any neighbors. I jumped in the window and landed on Jethro, who was still awake. "What happened?" he said. "Don't ask!" I replied, "Go to sleep!"

Caiaphas of Jerusalem

OUR PLAN SEEMS TO be working so far. Now it is up to Pilate to send that pretender from Galilee to the cross. I, myself, would have preferred stoning—much quicker. But we no longer have that choice. Annas is certain that he can convince Pilate to charge him with sedition—his claiming to be a king. What a travesty—Yeshua of Nazareth, King of Israel! The Sanhedrin has already convicted him of blasphemy, but that means nothing to Pilate. He must be convinced that this so-called Rabbi is disloyal to Rome and to the Emperor. If Pilate wavers, we may have to stir up the crowd to call for his crucifixion. They can shout, "Crucify! Crucify!" and "We have no king but Caesar!" That ought to do it. Pilate does not like to get involved with our disputes and thinks our religion is troublesome. However, he does not like disorder, and he knows this Rabbi has already caused a stir at the Temple and the crowds flock to him. We must make sure that Pilate sees him as a threat to society.

The Sanhedrin has known about this young man from Capernaum for a long time. Several years ago, we received a report from a Pharisee from Tiberias that this so-called Rabbi was going about preaching and teaching a message that was contrary to our Torah and traditions. He was known as a healer and even claimed to have the power to forgive sins. I remember that the man from Tiberias was very upset, and I was afraid he would have a heart attack. He continued to bring us reports, and we sent Scribes and Elders to test this young Rabbi. They all came back with both admiration and anxiety. They were impressed with the young Rabbi's grasp of Torah, and especially the Psalms and Prophets. They could not convince him that his interpretations were wrong. In fact, many times they could not answer his questions and arguments. His popularity among the poor and outcast, the lepers, blind, and lame is immense. He would have us believe we would be more obedient to Adonai if we practiced mercy rather than cleanness, that our insistence on purity is of no value if we do not show love to all people—and I am sure he means ALL people, even Samaritans and Gentiles. We are told that he even consorts publicly with prostitutes and tax collectors. How can one who claims to be Messiah sully himself with such contacts! Such blasphemy and blatant twisting of the Torah cannot be tolerated. He must be silenced for good.

Thankfully, we have our own supporters who have been able to bring him to justice before our tribunal. We were able to infiltrate his disciples and even convince one of them to betray him and help with his arrest. I think his name was Judas. We paid him a small sum for his work. Silver always outweighs loyalty. He helped our guards identify him. We did not want any mistakes. I heard from another priest that the disciple Judas had a change of heart and returned the money earlier tonight. Too bad—he did that all for nothing then. I also heard that another of his disciples cut off the ear of Malchus, my servant. I also heard that this Rabbi healed him and put his ear back on his head. I don't believe it. I think it was by Beelzebul that he mesmerized those present. It never really happened—just like a lot of those so-called healings he claims to have made. At any rate he was arrested, tried, and found guilty. It was easy. When I asked him if he was the anointed one, the messiah of Adonai, he said, "Yes! I am!" He then went on a rant about the coming Son of Man and the angels of heaven and judgment. For dramatic effect, I even tore my robes when I declared him guilty. Now he is off to Pilate for his condemnation.

I am still worried about how Pilate will deal with him. I think we need another plan to make sure Pilate sends him to death. We have a tradition that at Passover, one prisoner is released as a sign of the mercy of the Roman rule. Even this Rabbi cannot object to showing mercy. Isn't that what he is always preaching? We need to spread the word among our followers that they should ask for the release of another prisoner. But which one?

Simon of Capernaum

MY HEAD HURTS! MY heart hurts! My soul hurts! Last night was the worst night of my life. And here I am, somewhere in the outskirts of Jerusalem. The sun is just rising in the east. My head really hurts! So, what did I expect from all that wine I drank last night? What else was I to do after what I did? After I told everyone that I did not even know my Rabbi. I was afraid, but that was no excuse. He used to call me "Kephas," the rock. Some rock I turned out to be. At the first chance I get, I deny that I even know him. Somehow, I have to find him again and beg his forgiveness. Not once, not twice, but three times I said I was not one of his disciples—I was not with him. Strange, but he even knew this would happen. When I told him yesterday that I would follow him anywhere on earth, he frowned and said that before the cock crowed, I would deny him three times. I laughed it off, but deep inside I knew I wasn't as strong as I believed.

I don't even know where I am—somewhere in Jerusalem, near this ancient wall that does not seem to go anywhere. There is the broken wine jug I threw down when it was empty. There is the jagged hole in the wall that I hoped was not really there, but it was. I remember falling down next to it and crying like a baby. I remember calling out to Adonai: "Why did they have to capture him and arrest and abuse him? Him, of all people! He was your chosen one! How could you let this happen?" How could I let this happen? I tried to defend him in the garden! I cut off this man's ear! And what did he do? He healed him! And he told me to stop the violence! That was when we all ran—all except Judas. I never thought I would see him again. Last night I was pissing next to the hole in the wall when I heard someone. Someone was on the other side of the wall. I whispered, "Who's there? Who are you?" There was no answer, so I looked through the hole and there he was—there was Judas. I cursed him and tried to reach through the hole to get ahold of him. I wanted to break his neck. When I realized I couldn't reach him, I cried out, "Why Judas? Why did you do it? How much did they pay you, you traitor!"

I gave up trying to reach him and sat down and kept weeping. After some silence, Judas said, "I just wanted him to show himself, to declare who he was and then bring the army of angels and the Son of Man—Judgment Day, the Day of Adonai—like the prophets said would happen. Remember what they said? A day like no other, a day of unquenchable fire, a day of separation of good and evil, sheep and goats, weeds and wheat. Do you remember?" I shook my head and said, "Yes. I remember. But that was not for you to do. That was for Adonai to accomplish." Judas continued, "I thought that if I pushed him, if I exposed his enemies, he would do something. I never expected him to just let them take him away and, well, who knows what will happen to him now?" I asked him again, "How much did they pay you?" Judas whispered, "Thirty pieces of silver." Then he cried, "But I gave it back. They wouldn't take it, so I threw it into the Temple. It was blood money. They want to kill him! They want Pilate to crucify him!"

We were both silent for a while. Then Judas said, "I can never be forgiven for what I have done. I deserve to die." I then told Judas that I, too, had betrayed Rabbi Yeshua. I told him how I had denied him three times last night. I then told him I knew that somehow, I would be forgiven; somehow, I would find a way to tell Rabbi Yeshua what I had done, and he would forgive me. I just knew it. Judas then said, "Not for me! There is no way that I can be forgiven. It is impossible. I am unforgiveable. I am not worthy to live any longer." It was then that I saw he had a rope in his hand. "What are you going to do with that rope?" I asked. "What do you think!" he replied. "There is a big tree over there—just the right size—with a strong limb for a strong rope." "No" I said. "Don't do it! You can be forgiven—you can be. There is a way. There is always a way. Remember how Rabbi Yeshua always found a way to forgive people. He taught us to always be merciful, loving. Remember when I asked him if I had to forgive my brother seven times and he said 'No. Not seven times, but seventy times seven.' He will forgive you. I know he will. I do. I forgive you, Judas! Just don't do it." Before I knew it, he had stood up and run to the tree and tied the rope around the limb and then around his neck and jumped. I tried to break through the hole in the wall, but it was too late. I could only weep some more as I watched him sway in the distance.

Zilpah of Joppa

JERUSALEM AT PASSOVER! IT is the best time for begging of all the festivals. It is especially good among the pilgrims. I think they want to feel holy so they are more than willing to part with a few extra denarii. Yesterday was a pretty good day and today is the day before Passover so it ought to be even better. I've got my place all staked out—right here next to the Gate by the Temple. I can't stop thinking about that poor guy they hauled in last night. I wonder if he is still alive. Probably not, since everyone was against him. Even Pilate gave in to that nasty crowd. What does he care! He's not one of us. He's just a puppet of Rome and out for himself. What does he care if a few innocent Jews have to die to keep the peace? He probably brags about it to the Emperor.

Last night I was with some other beggars in the courtyard outside the high priest's place. They had built a fire in the middle of the courtyard and I was getting ready to roast something to eat. Suddenly there was some loud shouting and a group of guards and men with clubs came rushing in. They had some guy all tied up and were pushing him forward. He looked like he had been beaten. One guard called into the house and a young servant girl came out. They talked and then she went back inside. I sidled up to one of the guards and said, "You want some fish? Came all the way from Joppa—the best you can find." "Sure," he said as I handed him a chunk. "Who's the poor guy they've got all tied up?" He said, "Oh some Rabbi from Galilee. It seems he caused quite a stir at the Temple a few days ago. He's a troublemaker so the high priest wants to question him." "Yeah! I heard about that. He threw over some tables of those thieving moneychangers and let some animals loose. Must have been quite a riot. Looks like he got beat up pretty good." The guard smirked and said, "He must have fallen down while resisting arrest. They say he is a miracle worker, too. I'd like to see him get out of those ropes. That would be some miracle. All I know is that the crowds of poor and outcast just love him. They even think he is a messiah, even the new King of Israel, like some born-again David. I think the high priest is just jealous because he is not, I repeat, not so popular." The door opened again and the servant girl came back out. The guard said, "Thanks for the fish," and walked away.

The other guards picked up the poor, beaten Rabbi and pushed him through the door to the high priest's house. The servant girl came over to the fire and was warming herself when she suddenly pointed to a tall man around the fire. "You are one of his disciples, aren't you? I saw you with him." The tall man pulled his robe more tightly around him, and said, "I don't know what you are talking about. I don't know that man." As soon as he opened his mouth, I knew he was a Galilean. He had an accent. Somebody else also noticed: "You must be one of his friends. You have a Galilean accent." The tall man said again, "I tell you I do not know the man. Leave me alone!" Another in the crowd also accused him, saying that he remembered him from the riot at the Temple. The tall man backed away and yelled, "I do not know who that man is. I have never been with him," In the distance, a rooster crowed. The tall man looked like he had been struck by lightning. It was only a cock crowing. I didn't realize it was almost dawn. The tall man turned and ran into the night.

I thought that was the end of it. But I was wrong. In the morning, the guards came out, followed by the high priest and the scribes and elders. "We are taking him to Pilate," called one of them. "He is guilty of blasphemy and he must be sentenced to death." With that, they pushed that poor man onto the path to Pilate's headquarters. The crowd followed. So I went too— always ready for a good execution. As we walked along, I asked one of the Temple guards what had happened. He told me, "They questioned him for a long time and the young Rabbi said hardly anything in his defense. There were some who gave testimony against him—inciting a riot, threatening to destroy the Temple, stirring up the crowds—but they were all stooges giving false testimony. Finally, Caiaphas asked him directly, 'Are you the Messiah of Adonai?' and the fool said, 'Yes! I am' and then went on a rant about the coming of the Son of Man and all his angels—judgment day. Caiaphas then ripped his robe and said, 'You heard him. What more do we need? He must die for this blasphemy.' So here we are on our way to Pilate, since he is the only one who can condemn someone to death."

We stopped outside Pilate's headquarters while the Temple guards handed the young Rabbi over to the Romans. Caiaphas made a big deal of not going into the Roman palace to remain pure for the Passover. We all waited for Pilate to come out. Meanwhile, some of the High priest's people circulated in the crowd handing out coins and saying that when Pilate comes out, we are to shout for him to crucify the young Rabbi: "His name is Yeshua." I took some coins, but I wasn't about to shout for anybody to be crucified. Finally, Pilate came out with the young Rabbi, now stripped and beaten some more. Pilate spoke: "I find no guilt with this man. I will set him free." Caiaphas shouted, "No! You must find him guilty. He blasphemed!" With that, several in the crowd began to chant, "Crucify him! Crucify him!" Pilate said "Why? What has he done? I am not interested in your blasphemy." Caiaphas said, "He calls himself a king, setting himself against Caesar." "Are you a king?" Pilate joked. Rabbi Yeshua said, "You say so." Pilate then got angry: "Don't you know that I have power over you—the power of life or death?" Rabbi Yeshua then said, "You have no power over me unless it has been granted to you from above. You are not the guilty one here, but those who handed me over to you." Caiaphas then said, "You have a tradition of releasing one prisoner during Passover. We ask you to do this for us." Pilate turned to the crowd and, laughing, said, "Here is Yeshua of Nazareth, the King of Israel. Shall I release your king for you?" But the crowd, who had been prepared beforehand, shouted, "No! Release Barabbas! We want Barabbas!" I did not shout because I knew this Barabbas was a murderer and a thief. But Pilate finally gave in and handed over the young Rabbi to his soldiers.

I watched as the soldiers made fun of him. They spun him around and then put on his head a crown of thorns and a dirty old purple robe. They laughed at him and knelt down before him saying "Hail to the King!" When they finally brought out the crosspiece for the cross and laid it on his shoulders, I turned and walked away through the crowd that was still chanting "Crucify! Crucify!" As I walked out toward the gate, I noticed the same tall man at the rear of the crowd. He was standing silently and was weeping. So, you were one of his disciples, I thought to myself. I decided not to say anything to him. What could I say, anyway? I found my spot by the gate and put some dirt on my face to look more pitiful. I took off my shoes and hid them. Then I sat down and held out my bowl: "Alms for the poor! Alms for the poor!"

Marcus Pontius Pilate of Caesarea

I AM REALLY TIRED of this place and these troublesome people. I would much rather be back in southern Italy, at my family estate. But here I am in Judaea of all places. Caesarea is nice with the sea and the cool breezes and the wonderful food and wine. But Jerusalem is always trouble, besides being hot and dry. I also prefer to hunt down bandits and thieves, especially these sicarii who have murdered many of my best soldiers. We had one of them in prison just this week, but I had to release him because the people wanted him, this Barabbas, instead of that poor excuse for a king—the Rabbi from Galilee. I much rather would have sent that butcher Barabbas to the cross instead of that Yeshua—poor peasant. I still can't figure out what he had done to get the Sadducees so worked up. They say he claims to be like their god, a special envoy, even a chosen prophet or something like that. Oh, those Galileans can be trouble. They think because they are so far from Jerusalem that they can do what they want. Well, I showed them what it means to disrespect Rome. I sent in some troops on Passover a few years ago, killed a few of them while they were at worship. Maybe I went too far. Fortunately, there is no legate in Syria right now, so I can pretty much do as I wish. Anyway, the Sadducees and Caiaphas didn't care. With them, I have an understanding. They help me out and I keep them, especially Caiaphas, in power in Jerusalem. They even helped pay for my new aqueduct with some of their Temple treasury.

This Galilean, though, was a puzzle. He wasn't afraid of me or what I could do to him. He even told me I had no power unless it was granted by his god. What a joke! To think that his god is more powerful than the gods of Rome. I told him if his god is so strong, then why are we Romans ruling over you Jews. He told me that his kingdom is not of this world; if it were, his followers would fight. I said to him, "So, you are a king!" He said, "My kingdom is one of peace and justice and mercy. It is not like other kingdoms." I said, "Good luck with that!" I felt sorry for him. He was unrealistic and naïve, but he was not a threat. I wanted to release him. I thought if I let my soldiers make fun of him and rough him up, well, I thought that would satisfy the Jews and their Sanhedrin. I guessed wrong. "No!" they told me. "We have had our trial, and he is guilty of blasphemy and he has to die." Then they added, "He is also a threat to Rome because he claims to be a king, and we have no king but Caesar." That's a lie! They want to get rid of us and rule themselves. I think this Rabbi Yeshua is a threat to them, not to Rome. I think they are jealous that he has such a big following among the people, not only in Galilee, but here in Judaea. I asked this Rabbi why the Sadducees hated him so much; what had he done? He said nothing. He refused to defend himself. I was amazed, because he left me no choice.

So, I had my soldiers beat him up and make a mockery of his being a king. The crown of thorns was an especially good joke. Then I told the crowd that I could find no crime worthy of death, and that I would honor my practice of releasing a prisoner at Passover. When I said I would release Yeshua, they screamed their disapproval, and I could see the Sadducees stirring them up. What a bunch of crazies! I said, "Then who do you want me to release?" The crowd shouted, "Barabbas! Release Barabbas!" They were well coached. "Then what shall I do with this Galilean?" "Crucify him!" they screamed. "Crucify him!" I had no choice but to hand him over to be flogged and then crucified. And, of course, I had to release Barabbas. I told the captain of the guard to have a couple of soldiers follow Barabbas so we could arrest him later—or maybe just kill him.

I watched the soldiers push that young Rabbi out into the street. They seemed to enjoy these crucifixions. I did not wait for them to bring out the cross piece for him to carry up the hill. I've seen enough of these gruesome executions to last a lifetime. I went back into the palace. At least that is the last we will see of that Galilean and any more troublemakers. It was too early for wine, so I asked for some water and dates. I can't wait to get back to Caesarea for some decent fish. I will have to speak with Caiaphas before I leave, just to make sure he knows he owes me a big favor sometime in the future. I will speak with him on Sunday morning when things have settled down.

Aristobulus, Roman Centurion of Ephesus

I SURE HOPE THAT my mother doesn't have to watch me die a slow, painful death. That poor Jew on the Cross. His mother has been watching him for over an hour now. She came after he had been nailed to the cross and asked to speak with him. One guard came and asked if it would be alright to let her come closer. I said, "Yes." but I really wanted to send her away. She was with another young man who was visibly in grief. I mean, who wouldn't be. It is a terrible way to die. I went to escort her up to the place they call "The Skull," an apt name. She was quite strong looking and stood erect and walked with, well, with dignity. She reminded me of my mother, back in Ephesus with my two children. She, too, is strong and dignified. The young man with her was the one who needed help. When they got to the foot of the cross, she called his name—"Yeshua!" He looked down on them and smiled—at least he tried to smile. Then he said, "Mother. Take care of my friend." She put her arm around the young man, who wept even more. She said something in Aramaic and then turned away and helped the young man back down the hill. I noticed that there were some other women watching from a distance. I doubt they were friends of the other two criminals on the crosses. I watched the young man in the middle for a few more minutes and then went back to my station.

I think the Judean sun is finally getting to my brain. I am feeling sorry for these poor people. It was mid-morning when they were put up on their crosses. It had been at least three hours and the heat was getting to me. I took my cudgel, the symbol of my office, and whacked myself several times on my thigh—the one with all the scars. I looked at this cudgel and wondered where these vines had come from before they were twisted into this stick. I don't remember where I was stationed when I received it; every centurion gets one to mark their rank. Maybe it was in Syria, or maybe in Galatia. At any rate, it came in handy whenever I needed to wake up a sentry or threaten some poor peasant who wasn't paying his taxes. I whacked my thigh one more time and felt better, or at least more aware of the scene before me. There were three men on crosses; there were twenty soldiers standing guard; there were eight or ten people looking on at a distance. Just another day in Judea. What a place! And then, of course, there was the afternoon sun. Maybe it will hasten the deaths of those being crucified.

After another hour went by, I noticed a group of men coming up the hill. As I expected, the high priest and some of his entourage had finally deigned to make an appearance. They really have it in for the young man in the middle—I think his mother called him "Yeshua." I know he was responsible for the riot at the Temple last week, but that is hardly cause for a death sentence. Annas and Caiaphas have a lot of influence with Pilate, so they must have wanted him dead and gone for their own reasons. I understand he is very popular with the crowds, especially the poor and lower classes, which is about most of the people of Judea and Galilee. The soldiers say that he claims to be some kind of king, which is why they cloaked him all up in purple and put a crown of thorns on his head. I suppose they must have their fun. Pilate even put a sign on his cross: JESUS OF NAZARETH—KING OF ISRAEL. He had the inscription written in Latin, Greek and Hebrew, so everyone could read it. Pilate does have a cruel sense of humor. What I can't understand is why he agreed to release Barabbas and crucify this other one. Barabbas is a rebel, one of those sicarii who love to kill Romans. We will only have to hunt him down and arrest him again before he kills one more of my legion.

I watched as Caiaphas and some others came up to the crosses and mocked this Yeshua: "So, you are the Messiah. Then why don't you come down from the cross? Save yourself! Come down and then we will see and believe. Oh, maybe you can't—too bad!" They looked at each other laughing and said, "He saved others, but he cannot save himself." One of the two criminals next to him called out, "Yeah! Save yourself and save us too!" The other criminal told him, "Shut up! We are getting what we deserve. But this man is innocent." Then he turned to the Jew in the middle and said, "Remember me when you come into your reign." The young Jew said to him, "Today you will be with me in paradise." I almost laughed. What a dreamer he is. Suddenly some dark clouds came from out of nowhere and covered the sun. I thought it might even rain, but it was a relief from the heat, anyway. Strange. And it seemed to make everyone nervous. Everyone was silent. One priest came over to me and said, "What if they do not die before sundown when the sabbath begins. They cannot stay on the cross after that. Will you break their legs to make sure they die?" I just shook my head and turned away. The darkness continued for a few more hours. It made my soldiers uneasy. It made me wonder if this Yeshua was, I don't know, someone special. The priests from the Temple had all left. There was only one older man still standing below the crosses, looking at Yeshua. I walked over to him and asked if he knew this man. He said, "Yes. I know him. He is a great teacher and prophet. He is mistreated and abused, as were all the great prophets." I said nothing.

Suddenly, with great effort, the young man took a great breath and cried out something in Aramaic. I looked at the old man next to me and said, "What is he saying? What does he want?" The old man said, "He is quoting one of our Psalms: 'Eli, Eli, lema sabachthani.' It means 'My God! My God! Why have you forsaken me?'" I laughed and said, "Well, I can sure understand why he feels abandoned. Look at him. Innocent, but dying on a cross." The old man said, "Yes, so it seems. But the rest of the Psalm is a hymn of praise and hope—above all hope." I looked at the old man in disbelief. "Where's the hope in a cross?" I asked. He said nothing. It was then that we both noticed that he had stopped breathing. I turned away and said, "Well, it's all over." The old man said, "Or, maybe it is just beginning." I didn't know what to say, so I said, "Surely this man was a child of your God." The old man then said, "My name is Joseph of Arimathea. I have already spoken with Pilate and he has granted me permission to remove the body of Yeshua and place it in a tomb that I own. I need your permission as well." I nodded my approval. He turned and signaled to some women who had been keeping watch at some distance. They all came up the hill. I ordered two of my legionnaires to remove the body from the cross and give it to this Joseph and the women. Before he left, Joseph came to me and thanked me for my kindness. That was the first time anyone had ever thanked me for standing beneath a cross.

Simon of Kerioth, Father of Judas

I CAN'T BELIEVE THAT I am here outside Jerusalem, sitting next to my son's grave. I can't believe that the Sabbath is just ending and I am not at home with the rest of my family resting. I can't believe that I broke the Sabbath by traveling all night and now am defiled because I have touched—held—embraced a dead person. But he was my son. At least now he is buried in a shroud and his hands and feet tied properly and his face covered. At least now he has been blessed and lamented. Sadly, he is buried in a potter's field along with many others who could not be buried in a proper cemetery in Jerusalem. I wonder how many of these unknowns committed suicide? I can hardly believe it. What will I tell his mother? What will I tell the people of Kerioth? What will I tell myself? Truly, this is a field of blood. Speaking of blood, I have to find a way of washing myself.

It all happened so quickly. On Friday afternoon, a distant cousin arrived from Jerusalem. We were preparing for the Sabbath rituals and meal when he arrived. I could tell from the look on his face that something was terribly wrong. He asked to speak with me privately and then told me that my son Judas was dead and that I should come to Jerusalem at once. I said, "But it is almost the Sabbath and we cannot travel that far." "But you must," he said. "I will tell you on the way." He paused and then said, "Adonai will forgive." I quickly packed a few things and told my wife, "Judas is in trouble in Jerusalem and I must go to help him." She began to cry and said, "I knew it. I knew it. I knew he would find trouble with that Rabbi from Galilee. First it was Qumran; then it was that John the Baptizer; then that Rabbi—that troublemaker." Our two daughters came to her side and embraced her. "I will be back in a few days," I said, as I backed out the door.

We began the long walk north. While we walked, my cousin filled me in on what had happened. He told me how this young Rabbi was arrested and taken to the high priest. Judas was with them when he was arrested, but none of the other followers were taken into custody. He didn't know why, but for some reason Judas had taken his own life. He had hung himself. Out of fear? Was he despondent? I was stunned and then asked him where his body was. Had he been buried? Where? Who had taken care of his body? Who were the other disciples? Where could they be found? To all these questions, my cousin had no answers. He was acquainted with one disciple named Thaddeus, who came and told him about Judas' death. He had left Jerusalem for Kerioth early on Friday in order to tell me. I thanked him and then felt so dizzy I had to stop and take some water. We kept walking and arrived in Jerusalem at dawn on Saturday.

My cousin took me to his house and gave me something to eat and suggested that I go to the Roman headquarters where there was a morgue. I thanked him and began my search for my son. I approached the Roman soldiers outside the fortress and said, "My name is Simon and I am looking for my son's body." The soldier looked at him with disinterest and said, "What makes you think he is here, in our morgue?" I told him he had died suddenly and that I just assumed he would be here. "What's his name?" "Judas," I told him, "Judas." The heat of the day made me dizzy. "Judas what?" the soldier said, clearly annoyed. "Iscariot," I said, "Judas Iscariot." Suddenly, one legionnaire rose from his chair with the clear sound of metal armor clinking. Another soldier put his hand on his sword. "No." I said. "No! It is not what you think. The name has nothing to do with the sicarii—the Zealots. It comes from the name of our town, Kerioth, south of here, near Hebron."

"So, you are a Jew. Why come to us then? Do we look Jewish?" The soldier looked around and received the appropriate snorts of laughter from the others. "Why don't you go over to the Temple and ask your 'own' people where your son's body might be. They take care of all the Jewish bodies. We just get the riffraff and the strangers." I remember how ashamed I was and told them that my son had committed suicide so he could not be buried in a traditional Jewish way. "What did he look like?" asked one soldier. "He was about 20 years old, reddish hair, not much of a beard, medium build—and probably dressed in a nice tunic—Judas liked expensive clothes." I watched as he got up and went out a side door. Another legionnaire came over and said, "You look out of place here in Jerusalem, but you did seem to know something about the sicarii." "Yes," I said. "My eldest son was one of them. He is dead, too, killed in an attack on a Roman patrol near Caesarea Philippi. And my youngest son is in prison for smuggling weapons. And now

Judas." I was ready to faint when the legionnaire grabbed me and led me to a bench. He asked me what Judas was doing in Jerusalem, assuming he was here for Passover, no doubt. "Terrible way to have things end up."

I told the legionnaire that Judas had become obsessed with finding the Messiah, the one who would bring in a new way of life and restore Israel to its former greatness. First, he went to Qumran, near the Dead Sea, and then he was with a man named John, a self-described prophet. Finally, he ended up in Galilee with a young Rabbi named Yeshua. He was with him for almost three years. We saw little him, but he was sure that this Rabbi was the messiah and was soon going to bring in the new kingdom of Israel. Apparently, he was wrong because I am told that this Rabbi Yeshua was just crucified yesterday. I guess Judas just couldn't cope with the failure. The legionnaire shook his head and said that he had been present when this Rabbi was crucified. He told me they had been watching him and his followers because they had caused a riot at the Temple a week ago. He then said that his Centurion even knew where they were all hiding. Just then the other legionnaire came back and said, "Sorry. There is no one who matches your son's description." I then asked the friendlier legionnaire if he would ask his superior to tell me where I could find the Rabbi's followers. He left the room and was gone for almost an hour. When he came back, he quietly told me where to look in the city, an old section called the "City of David," in an upper room near the city wall.

I wasn't very hopeful, but I began to search the city, asking people where the old City of David section was. I finally found it and began knocking on doors, looking for an upper room somewhere. By midafternoon I was getting discouraged. When I knocked on an old door, it was opened by a young man. I told him who I was and asked if there was a man named Thaddeus in the house. He looked surprised and said, "Wait here." I could hear him running up the stairs. A few moments later, the door re-opened. A man stood there and said, "I am Thaddeus." I told him I was Simon, Judas' father, and that he knew my cousin who had come to Kerioth to bring me to Jerusalem, and that I needed to find where my son was buried. He looked at the ground and then up and down the street. He then said, "Wait here. I will be back." After a few minutes, he returned and introduced me to another man named Phillip, who was carrying a shovel. They stepped into the street and said to follow them. We left the city and entered the Valley of Hinnom. Thaddeus said that this was the place where many poor and outsiders were buried. He looked at me with pain in his eyes: "I'm sorry. We didn't know where else to bury him."

The two disciples walked around for a short time, looking at the ground and the newly turned earth. Philip said, "Here! This is the place." Thaddeus agreed, and they started to dig. "It is not too deep," Philip said. "But it will not be pleasant." Three feet down they stopped and I could see the shape of a body. I jumped into the grave and pulled and pushed the dirt aside. I pulled the shroud away and could see clearly. It was Judas. I pulled him to me, brushing the dirt from his hair and beard. I cried out in grief and rocked back and forth, holding my son. I held him close for many minutes before I realized I was now defiled for touching a dead person. I looked around and was glad that there was no one else but Thaddeus and Philip. I stroked his face and lowered him again into the grave. I said the words to the only Psalm I could think of: "Here my cry, Adonai, and listen to my prayer." I replaced the shroud and tied his hands and feet and placed a cloth over his face after I had kissed his forehead. I climbed out of the grave and Philip shoveled in the dirt again. I sat down and wept—for me, for his mother, for his family.

We sat there for a few more minutes and then I asked, "What happened? Do you know anything?" Thaddeus told me that one of the other disciples, Simon, saw it happen. He had tried to talk Judas out of doing anything, but he couldn't reach him in time. It happened on Thursday night, after Rabbi Yeshua was arrested. "Judas had left us earlier in the evening, so none of us saw him until the arrest in the garden. We could not figure out why Judas was there with the Temple guards, and we could not hear what he said. We only know that when he kissed Rabbi Yeshua, the guards grabbed him and took him away. We all became frightened and ran, so we never saw him again. The next morning, Simon told us what had happened and Philip and I came and found him hanging from a tree near the Jerusalem wall. We decided then to bury him here. I guess we are defiled, too." I said, "Thank you for helping." Philip then said, "Our Rabbi, Yeshua, always said that love and mercy are more important than keeping pure. He touched dead people—even brought some back to life. He touched lepers in order to heal them. He often let unclean people touch him. He wasn't afraid. So, I guess we shouldn't be afraid either. Clearly you loved your son, so embracing him, even though he is dead, is a sign of love. I think Adonai understands."

Thaddeus and Philip invited me to join them for dinner, but I said I wanted to find my cousin and tell him what happened. I asked them what they would do without their Rabbi. They looked at each other and said, "We don't know? Some will go back to Galilee. Some will keep preaching and sharing what he taught us. We still have to go to the tomb tomorrow to make sure he is properly buried. His mother is upstairs and is distraught." I dread the trip back to Kerioth. What will I tell his mother? What will I tell his friends? What will I tell myself? Whatever happens, I hope that the message of love and mercy that I heard from their Rabbi continues to grow and find a home in the world. I know I will look at my world differently from now on. Maybe that is what I can take away from the tragedy of Judas' death. I offered both thanks and a blessing as they walked away, back to Jerusalem, back to mourn another death.

Saturday Night in the Upper Room

Simon of Capernaum

TOMORROW WE WILL BE able to give him a decent anointing and burial. We know where he is buried and some of the women have agreed to go early in the morning to make sure he is cared for. If there is a problem with the stone at the entrance, they will come back and a few of us can remove it. I thought tonight we could all take a turn and remember something special, something he said or did that is important to us. There are so many things that I can think of beginning with how he healed my mother-in-law to how he knew he was going to die, but was unafraid. One thing that always amazed me was how he could look inside of someone and somehow know what that person was thinking or what they were really like. I remember this young man came running up to him one day and asked what he had to do to inherit eternal life. Yeshua looked, not just at him, but into him, and somehow saw that he was trapped by his wealth and possessions. I remember the young man was dressed in really nice clothes and had several rings on his hands. Yeshua looked into this young man and truly loved him. And then he said to him, "Give away all your possessions to the poor, and come and follow me." I still remember how sad and miserable that young man looked when he stood up and walked away. I guess he couldn't part with his money and his stuff. I remember then that Rabbi Yeshua said, "It is very hard for a rich person to get into the good graces of Adonai. It is easier for a camel to go through the eye of a needle than for a rich person to get into heaven." We all laughed. But I was upset because I suddenly realized that none of us is really worthy. I said to him, "Who then can be saved?" He smiled and said that it is impossible for us to save ourselves. And then he said, "Fortunately for us, with Adonai all things were possible." I remember he looked around at each of us. I think he was looking inside each of us.

He looked inside me not long ago and told me I would deny him three times before the cock crowed—and I did. I did! I denied I even knew him because I was afraid. I had followed him into the courtyard of the high priest's house and someone recognized me and I denied I was one of his disciples. I don't know why, but I know he will find a way to forgive me. I know that sounds foolish and even self-serving, but I believe it. Somehow, I must find a way to continue his life, his work, his promise of Adonai's mercy and love for everyone. He wanted us to become preachers—to spread his words. Sometimes I don't think I would be a very good preacher, at least not like him. I think after tomorrow, I will go back to Galilee and go fishing. Maybe that will help clear my head and make sense of all this tragedy and violence and shame. At least I know I am good at casting nets and mending sails. I am good at fishing, but I am not sure about preaching.

Andrew of Capernaum

AND YOU WERE NOT very good at walking on water, either. I will never forget the look on your face when you tried to walk on Gennesaret and began to sink. You were petrified. Fortunately, Rabbi Yeshua was there to help you climb back into the boat. That was quite a day. I remember we had gone out in the boat and left him on the shore. A strong wind had come up, and we were having trouble steering back to the beach. The waves kept pushing us farther out when we saw someone walking on the water—or so we thought. One of us said, "Look! It is a ghost!" We were all startled when we heard his familiar voice: "It is I. Do not be afraid!" He said that a lot. Then big, brave Simon stood up and said, "Lord, if it is you, command me to come to you on the water." Then he got over the side and none of us could believe it. Old Simon was walking on top of the water. But he made the mistake of looking down at the waves, and he got scared—poor Simon. He began to sink and cried for help: "Lord, save me!" And, of course, he did. Rabbi grabbed you by the arm and hauled you back on board. Then he got into the boat, too. I remember he sat down and the wind suddenly ceased blowing. He looked around and said, "Why did you doubt? Have you so little faith?" He said that a lot, too.

It was crazy enough that he could walk on water. But when the wind stopped blowing, we were all dumbfounded. For me, that was proof that he was someone special, someone unique. Messiah? Son of Man? Miracle worker? I was not sure what title to give him. I only know that he had powers that set him apart from everyone I had ever known. After that day, I was certain that we were all part of something new and life-changing. I certainly did not expect it to end with his being crucified like a common criminal, but I will continue to live with the hope of the coming reign of Adonai. The greatest thing that I took away from that day on the lake, other than Simon's surprised face, is Rabbi Yeshua's words: "Do not be afraid!"

Mary, Mother of James

WHAT I REMEMBER MOST about him was the way he treated children. Maybe it's because he was always so nice to my own grandchildren. He always had a kind word for them. He never ignored them or seemed to find them bothersome. He treated them with-well, with respect. I am just sorry that he never had children of his own. But that is a different story, I suppose. I remember one day when he had come to our house. James' father had just come in from fishing and had gone to wash up. The grandchildren were eager to hear about the day on the lake. Rabbi Yeshua took them aside and told them about his own father, Joseph, and how he couldn't wait to hear about what his own father had done all day. His father was a carpenter and a stone worker. Rabbi told them about how his father had taught him how to cut wood to make doors and tables, and how he cut stone to make windows and other things. Then he took out a small knife from his belt and showed it to the children. He told them how his father had given it to him when he was ten years old and had taught him how to carve things with it. The children were fascinated. One of them asked, "What did you carve?" Rabbi Yeshua said the first thing he carved was a snake to scare the girls with. Then he made a bird and then a dog. He said he always carried the knife with him to remind him of his father. As soon as James' father came back, they all deserted him and ran to their grandfather.

Another time, he was teaching a group by the lake and some children came by. But you, disciples, shooed them away and told them to be quiet. When Rabbi Yeshua saw them, he stopped and called for the children to come to him. Of course, they all ran and jumped into his lap. After he had blessed them all, he picked up one little child and said to the crowd, "If you want to be one of Adonai's people, you must become like a little child. You must have faith like this child. You must become trusting like this child. Whoever does this will be the greatest in the kingdom. When you welcome a little child, you welcome me. And do not despise any of these little ones, for the angels in heaven are watching them—and they are watching you. So, do not ignore them or cause them to stumble and fall and be lost. Adonai has a special place for each of these little ones—and for you who love and care for them." I will always remember how kind he was with children, especially my own, James and John, who are not always easy to get along with. He named you well, "Boanerges."

James of Capernaum

I BLAME THAT NAME on John, my younger brother. He was the one who was always causing problems. I think what I will miss the most is his sense of humor. He would always add humor to his teaching and his rants, especially against the Pharisees. He was always calling them "blind guides" since they were the ones who were supposed to be the experts at seeing things. Of course, he often referred to us as blind too. "Don't you get it?" he would say to us. "Do you have eyes but don't see?" Like when he fed those thousands of people and we gathered up the twelve baskets of left-overs, and then when we were on the lake and we had forgotten to bring any bread, and he said, "Beware of the yeast of the Pharisees" and we thought he was talking about how we had no bread. He laughed out loud and said, "Why are you talking about having no bread? Are you blind, still? Adonai will always provide you with enough bread to eat, and to share. And Adonai will give you insight and courage, and the ability to understand the Torah, and to preach the good news which is the bread of life." Once he said to us, "Do you know what happens when a blind person leads another blind person?" One of us said, "They will get lost." "Yes," Rabbi replied. "And worse, they will both fall into the pit." Then he laughed—at least he thought it was funny.

One of the best jokes he told was when he said to us and the surrounding crowd: "I am the shepherd. And you all are the sheep." Now all of us knew about sheep. Anyone who has grown up in Palestine knows about sheep—they are dumb. Cute, but dumb. To be called a sheep is not what anyone wants to be called. I am sure that he said that with a smile, even though most of us did not get it at the time. We were all probably saying, "Well, no thank you. I would rather be the shepherd." His humor was a great way to keep us humble. I need to remember that. I think that if we are to continue the work of sharing Adonai's message, we will need to remember not only Rabbi's words and deeds, but his humor as well. I will need to take myself less seriously, as if I were the important one. That will be difficult for me, but it will be even more difficult for my brother John.

Philip of Bethsaida

To TELL YOU THE truth, I am scared, terrified even. This afternoon, Judas' father came to our door and Thaddeus and I took him to where we had buried Judas. He told us that the only way he had found us was because this Roman centurion knew where we were hiding. He said the Romans had been watching us ever since the riot at the Temple last week. They crucified Rabbi Yeshua! What do you think they might do to us, too? I try not to think about it. I try to remember the good times.

I agree with James. Rabbi Yeshua had a great sense of humor. It wasn't only his humor, though. It was the way he seemed to always turn the world upside down. How many times did he say: "The first shall be last and the last first?" And how many times did he make the 'respectable' or the 'religious' ones the villains of his stories, or the butt of his jokes and rants—yes, he did go on some wild rants now and then. At first it was confusing. But then I got the message that Adonai sees things very differently than we do. I couldn't believe it when he told the Pharisees that prostitutes and tax collectors would enter heaven before them. I had always thought of those pious people as the ones favored by Adonai. I remember one story about a rich man and a beggar, I think he called him Lazarus. The rich guy had everything—money, good food, a big house—and Lazarus had nothing, and sat in the dirt begging. The rich man passed him by every day and barely noticed him. Then they died. And it was the rich man who was tormented in Sheol. And Lazarus was at peace in Abraham's embrace. What a surprise! And the rich man couldn't even get a drop of water for his thirst. I remember how frightened I was that this might happen to me. Rabbi Yeshua made me very aware how important it was to care for everyone, especially the poor.

I think the sermon I will remember the most was when we were still in Galilee, and we went up to a high place with a large crowd of people. He sat down and the people gathered in close to listen. He talked a lot about being blessed, but very differently from what I had been taught. I always thought that blessings were things like money and prestige and safety and happiness. Rabbi Yeshua turned things upside down again. He said: "Blessed are you who are poor, for yours is the presence of Adonai. Blessed are you who are hungry, for you will soon be filled. Blessed are you who weep, for you will soon laugh." He went on: "Blessed are you who are meek, for you will inherit the earth." Now that one really stunned me because I always thought that power and might were what made you important. Then he said: "Blessed are you peacemakers, for you will be called children of Adonai." Nothing about purity and ritual and obeying the rules. Peacemaking was what did it. Then he finished with, "Blessed are you who are persecuted—persecuted for being righteous—for in you is the reign of Adonai." I knew then that following this man was going to be difficult and that I would have to be willing to lose my life if necessary. I think he knew all of this way back in Galilee and yet he kept going—all the way to the cross—another symbol of the world turned upside down.

Bartholomew of Cana

You may like the world turned upside down, but I like it ordered and dependable, like the seasons of the year and the workings of a farm. I like how the Torah describes the creation of everything by Adonai as "good," and absent of chaos, although the past few days have been full of disorder. I liked how Rabbi Yeshua explained things in terms of planting and harvesting, with seeds and nurture and even manure. Remember the time he told the parable of the man who planted a fig tree and it didn't produce any fruit and the owner was going to yank it out and burn it? But the gardener said, "Wait another year. Let me dig around it and put on some manure and see if it does better. Next year, if it is still fruitless, then we can dig it up and burn it." I liked that because sometimes we get so frustrated because people seem so hopeless and so stubborn about seeing what Adonai is doing. We sometimes expect people to get the good news immediately, and to change their ways just because we or Rabbi Yeshua says to change. I think it is good for us to remember to be more patient and kinder, and keep fertilizing the seeds we plant.

I also liked the way he used agriculture to paint a picture of the truth about the world. He told us all more than once that the seed falls on different soils, so we shouldn't expect the same results. Remember the parable of the rocky soil and the brambles and the good soil? All we are called to do is to keep spreading the seeds—the words and deeds of love and mercy and joy—and look for the harvest to come. He also warned us we will have enemies who will spread weeds while we are spreading wheat. He told us not only to expect this to happen, but again to be patient, and careful not to pull up the weeds for fear we will pull up the wheat, too. As a farmer, I know how challenging this can be. I know I am not always very patient. I guess my favorite image is the one of the mustard seed, the smallest seed we have. Rabbi told us that even though it is so small, when it is planted, and nurtured, and grows, it will spread out far and wide and provide a place for many birds to nest and find a home. That is what gives me hope.

Mary of Magdala

I LIKE ORDER, TOO. Maybe that is why I have done so well in the trading business. However, sometimes order—rules and regulations and codes of behavior—can become burdensome, even hurtful. I have always loved how Rabbi Yeshua taught embrace rather than exclusion. He practiced hospitality, not hostility. I know what it is like to be an outsider. My mother was Jewish, so, technically, that makes me Jewish as well. But my father was Persian. So, I became suspect. I was not quite pure enough. Maybe that is why so many men were unwilling to consider me as a wife. Maybe that is why I ended up marrying a Gentile. And that, too, made me suspect. You have all heard the many rumors about me—the loose woman, the half-breed seductress. I was never so happy as when Rabbi Yeshua welcomed me, just as I was.

I remember his many teachings about the Torah being meant to be a joy, a blessing. I also remember how often he criticized the Pharisees and Sadducees who had made it a burden. He said once that they have placed heavy obligations on everyone, and they will not lift a finger to ease them. He often challenged their rules because they injured people rather than helped them. One time he healed a man with a withered hand. He did it on the sabbath, in front of a group of Pharisees. I think he did it on purpose, just to get them upset. But the point he made was that doing good was more important than honoring the Sabbath. Another time he said to them, "You strain out a gnat and swallow a camel"—I couldn't help laughing to myself. I know he was furious because he had just told them they would follow the rules about tithing mint and dill and cumin, but forgot about justice and mercy and faith, which are far more important obligations of the Torah. He even went so far as calling them "whitewashed tombs," beautiful on the outside, but dead on the inside.

I also believe that he has made all of you better men—willing to see women as equals, or at least not as inferior, or as mere property. I know this has been difficult for many of you. I remember the time we were in Samaria, and you came upon him sitting by a well talking with a woman. She was doubly tainted, being both a woman and a Samaritan. But there he was, not only talking to her in public—how shameful—but accepting a drink of water from her own vessel—how unclean! Yet, she was the one who went into the town and convinced everyone that Rabbi Yeshua was the Messiah. He was regularly condemned for welcoming women as dinner guests, followers, even disciples. He defended women, even women condemned for adultery. That took great courage. And now he has paid the price for his love and embrace of all people. He broke the rules. For this he was broken. I pray we will continue his gift of radical hospitality, even if it means that we get broken as well.

John of Capernaum

I AM ANGRY! I am angry at the Romans! I am angry at the Jews, especially Caiaphas and the Sanhedrin. I am angry at myself, at us, because we all ran away. Simon was the only one who stood up to the soldiers. I wanted to, but I didn't. I like that Rabbi Yeshua got angry sometimes. Never violent! But often angry. Not only with his opponents, but frequently with us—maybe too often with us. We just didn't get it, did we? I guess I should just speak for myself. I just didn't get. I can't even blame James for that—I did it all myself. I remember one time he had been teaching in parables and when we were alone with him, someone asked why he taught in parables. He looked at us in dismay, and then he got angry and told us we had better understand these parables if we wanted to understand what Adonai had in mind for us and for the new world ahead. He told us that he spoke in parables to get us to think in new ways, but mostly just to think. I guess I was just lazy. It was difficult to change my thinking and my assumptions about life and other people.

I remember one time when we were going through Samaria and the people there would not welcome us. James and I wanted Rabbi Yeshua to call down fire from heaven and burn them all. We thought that was the right thing to do to that kind of people. But, he got mad at us. He said he wouldn't do it. That was embarrassing. I think I have learned that I can be angry and not be violent. Above all, I have learned that violence only makes things worse. Violence is easy—stupid—but easy. Non-violence is often more difficult and requires more courage and more patience. Rabbi Yeshua taught this and lived this. And it cost him his life.

I have also learned not to think of myself first. At the very beginning, he kept talking about the coming reign of Adonai in the world. James and I thought it would be good for us to be in top positions in this new kingdom. One day when we were alone, we asked Rabbi Yeshua if we could sit at his right and left side when he comes into his glory. He looked at us with both sadness and concern. He told us we did not really know what we were asking. Then he said, "Are you willing to drink the cup I will drink, and be baptized with the baptism I will receive?" We didn't really know what he was talking about, but we both said, "Yes, we are able." He shook his head and said that, indeed, we would drink the cup that he will drink and be baptized with the baptism he will receive. But he cannot grant our request. It was not for him to decide. I realized I had overstepped my place. I had put myself ahead of everyone else. I had been selfish. When the rest of you heard about our request, we were not the most popular disciples for a long time. Humility comes slowly for me. I am still working on it. Rabbi Yeshua is still teaching me.

Matthew of Tiberias

OF ALL OF YOU, I think I am the one least likely to be here. For most of my life I just found the way to get by, to look at each situation and figure out how I could benefit by it, how I could get the upper hand. When I saw a chance to get ahead, to gain both power and wealth, I did. I became a tax collector. I sold out my own people. The Romans were looking for local men to do their dirty work, and I was the one who stepped forward. I admit I did it with great fear and repugnance. But I got used to it. I enjoyed the money and the self-importance. Most people hated me. Even the Romans looked down on me. They knew I was a collaborator. They used me even though they despised me. I tried not to use force, even violence, but some-times I had to. I didn't want to, but I had to.

Then one day I was sitting at my collection table, in front of my nice house, and this man walked up and looked at me like he knew exactly who I was. He looked at me with compassion and gentleness. I knew who he was. It was my business to know about anyone who might be a threat to my work. I knew he was a teacher, a healer, and something much more. I expected him to judge me, to condemn me, to call me a traitor. But he just smiled and reached out his hand and said, "Follow me! Come with me and help bring in the reign of Adonai." I was stunned. I was embarrassed. I couldn't believe that he was serious. And then he smiled at me and put his hand on my shoulder. I wanted to cry, but instead I stood up and left the tax table and, and, here I am. I don't know what is next for me, for us. I only know that I am committed to finding a way to live that is forgiving and non-violent and true to the Torah. I will not go back to the life I once lived. I want to find a way to repay and help those that I wronged and cheated. I know it sounds crazy, but I want to find some good news in all of this. After all that Rabbi Yeshua did for me, I want to share some with others—even the Romans who used to order me around. Someone earlier said how he could turn the world upside down. Well, he certainly did that to me—and I am glad he did.

Shalomie of Nazareth

EXCEPT FOR HIS MOTHER, I have known Yeshua the longest. Mary and I were young mothers in Nazareth many years ago. Our children grew up together. Yeshua and his brothers and sisters were as much a part of my family as mine were of hers. We had often talked about him marrying one of my daughters, but it never happened. Maybe it is just as well. Sadness and loss seem to follow us around. I remember many stories about Yeshua as a young boy and a young man. I remember how proud he was of his father, who was an excellent carpenter, and a good husband and father. He often spoke of helping his father with wood and stone. He tried to show off by trying to lift a stone slab or a large timber. All the girls thought he was cute and so smart. And he was both cute and smart.

What I remember most about him was how inquisitive he was. He wanted to know how everything worked, and why. He was never satisfied with a simple answer. He drove his father crazy with questions. And our rabbi was always telling him, "That's enough, Yeshua. No more questions." When he was little, he used to play King David and Goliath. He would be King David, of course. And he would pester Hassan—the young man from Gaza who had come with Mary and Joseph and then stayed and married one of the young women of Nazareth—until Hassan agreed to play Goliath. Yeshua said it had to be somebody big and tall or it wasn't real. Hassan would stomp around threatening the children until Yeshua, as David came out and knocked him dead with a slingshot. It was great fun, and Hassan was very patient with the children, especially young Yeshua. Poor Hassan will be heartbroken when he hears what has happened.

I think what I will remember most about him was how patient and gentle he was with old people, especially if they were sick. Oh, that poor woman who had been sick for over twelve years; and that blind man in Jericho. He always had time for people like me. He would never be rushed when there was an elder that just needed a little more time, or a kind word, or just someone to sit with them. I guess none of us older folks thought he would die before we did. And we certainly did not think he would die in such a brutal and painful way. I will miss him like a son.

Thomas of Sepphoris

MAYBE WE WERE WRONG. Maybe we were just unrealistic. Maybe we let our hopes and dreams cloud our vision? Maybe we expected too much of him? I don't know! Sometimes I think he missed too many opportunities to make clear that Adonai had given him these incredible powers in order to renew Israel and bring in this new kingdom. More than once did the Pharisees and Sadducees demand a sign from him. "Show us," they demanded. "Give us a sign that you are the anointed one!" And he always refused. He could have had them on his side, and maybe then this whole tragedy could have been averted. He could have shown them what they wanted and then demanded that they change their ways. Instead, he tells them that the only sign they will get is "the sign of Jonah," whatever that means. Jonah was a malcontent who preached a message of doom. I know his message, like Rabbi Yeshua's, was one of repentance. But did he have to always remind the Jewish leaders that Adonai's mercy extends even to outsiders and enemies, like the Ninevites? It was like he was setting himself up as an outsider, when he could have reminded them he was a faithful follower of the Torah, like them.

Nobody wants a dead Messiah, much less one who was crucified like a common criminal. I love all of his teachings and his message of mercy and love to all people—even our enemies. I remember when I first heard him talking this way: "What's the big deal if you love those who love you? Even the non-Jews do that. What is the risk if you are kind to those who are kind to you? No, you are to love your enemies and pray for those who persecute you." I was speechless when I heard Mary tell us that, even on the cross, he refused to curse his enemies. He said, before he died, "Father, forgive them, for they do not know what they are doing." But we are going to have a difficult time convincing people that this message will change, much less renew, the entire world. We need some kind of proof. We will need more healings to show the power of Adonai. We will need a miracle, something never seen before, in order to convince people that what we are preaching is the way to behave, and the life that Adonai wants for us all.

James Ben Alpheus

MY GRANDMOTHER WAS BLIND, so I will always remember the many times Rabbi Yeshua healed blind people. The last one he healed was Bartimeus, in Jericho. Whatever happened to him? After he could see again, he followed us everywhere, even up to Jerusalem. I haven't seen him for days. Well, I remember one of the first people he healed. It was a small village in Galilee. Some people brought this young man to us and asked for help. Rabbi Yeshua took him outside the village and we watched as he spit on his fingers and rubbed the man's eyes. He asked the man if he could see anything, and the young man got very excited and said he could see light and shapes, but they all looked like trees. Rabbi spit on his fingers again and rubbed his eyes some more. He stepped back and I can still see the huge smile that came of that young man's face. "I can see! I can see! Everything is so beautiful!" And then he began to cry, and hugged Rabbi Yeshua so hard, I thought he would hurt him. Naturally, we were all amazed. Then he said we needed to go on to another village.

I also remember the way he taught us to see things, how Adonai sees them. I have an uncle who is a rabbi. His favorite prophet is Jeremiah. He would often tell us how Adonai had taught Jeremiah to see things. Shortly after Jeremiah agreed to be a prophet, Adonai gave him a vision: "What do you see?" he asked. Jeremiah could see the things that Adonai had in store for the people, even when the future was dim and full of struggles. Then my uncle would challenge us to look at the world with the eyes of Adonai. Rabbi Yeshua had those eyes. He could see things that few others could see. I remember one time he was teaching a large crowd, and he said, "Why do you see the speck that is in your neighbor's eye, but do not notice the log that is your own eye? Or how can you say, 'Here friend, let me take out the speck that is in your eye,' when you yourself do not see the log that is in your own eye? You are being a hypocrite. First take the log out of your own eye and then you will see clearly to take out the speck that is in your neighbor's eye." I will always remember this and hope that I can become more humble and less hypocritical. I will try to see the world with his eyes.

Thaddeus of Nain

I AM SURE BY now that you have all heard what happened this afternoon. Judas' father, Simon, showed up at our door and Philip and I took him to the grave of his son, out there in the Hinnom Valley. We did not expect it to be such an emotional time, but it was really tough, especially knowing what Judas had done on Thursday night. We did not tell his father. We made up some story about his being upset and frantic about Rabbi Yeshua's arrest, which, I guess, was true. At least we helped his father give Judas a proper burial. Let's hope we can do the same with Rabbi Yeshua.

I saw this all coming some months ago. I was worried that he was making too many powerful enemies and his criticism of the Temple and the Pharisees and Sadducees just kept getting more and more harsh. But I never thought that he would be handed over to the Romans, much less crucified by Pilate. He even warned us at least two or three times that he was going to be in danger of being tortured and killed. That was why I tried to convince him not to go up to Jerusalem. If we had stayed in Galilee, this would never have happened. He wouldn't listen.

He kept reminding us that prophets had to bring their message to Jerusalem, and that here was where the prophets were killed. I remember when we were approaching the city last week. I was walking next to him and noticed he was weeping. He said quietly, "Jerusalem! Jerusalem! You kill the prophets and stone those who are sent to you. How often I wanted to gather your children together as a mother hen gathers her chicks, but you refused. And so, your house will become desolate—not one stone will be left upon another." I really don't really think he wanted to die. I think he wanted the people to repent and change their ways. He came to give them all one last chance. Maybe that is why he was so harsh and critical of them. Maybe we, too, are supposed to keep reminding them of Adonai's message of mercy and forgiveness. I have never thought of myself as a mother hen, but I am willing to try.

Simon the Canaanite

I WILL ALWAYS REMEMBER the day when I decided to become a disciple. Rabbi Yeshua was in the upper Galilee, near Tyre, not far from where I lived. He healed the daughter of a Canaanite woman—he cast out her demon. He did it without actually being with her, just with a word. I never really knew the power of words until that day. Almost as important was him not rejecting this woman, even though she was not Jewish; she was an outsider. I know what it is like to be an outsider. Now I am an outsider, even in my own family. My father was very upset when I chose to follow Rabbi Yeshua. "He does not follow the traditions of our ancestors. He teaches as a false prophet. Yes!—he heals—but maybe by Beelzebul. Beware, my son! Beware!" My father will not understand, but some of my brothers are thinking differently. They even ask me about certain rules and laws. I have tried to be helpful and clear, but I know I have caused conflict in my family. I remember when Rabbi Yeshua said, "Who are my mother and my father and my relatives? The ones who do the will of Adonai—these are my mother and my sisters and brothers." I was drawn to him because he spoke so often about doing the right thing—about actions that match your words.

I remember recently he was preaching about the day of judgment. We were in Jerusalem, near the Temple, and naturally, there was a crowd around him. We were watching people place their gifts into the Temple treasury. Some of the wealthy people made a great show of their giving. Then an older woman came quickly to the place, and tried to disguise her gift of two copper coins, which she quickly dropped into the box. "There!" Yeshua said. "There was the greatest gift yet! This woman gave out of her poverty. For so many others, their gifts will not make them insecure, or possibly hungry, or even homeless. But this woman gave with faith." Then he went on to tell some parables about the day of judgment. The one I remember most clearly was about how people acted without thought of reward, without even realizing that they were acting with love and mercy. "When did we see you hungry and give you some food, or thirsty and give you something to drink? And when did we see you a stranger and welcome you, or naked and gave you clothing? And when did we see you sick or in prison and visit you?" And Rabbi Yeshua said, "As you did it to these, the least of my sisters and brothers, you did it to me." I thought of my grandmother who used to say, "Do good. Then go away." I still can't believe that this man who taught such humility and lived for others was crucified. He taught that acts of love fulfill the Torah, that mercy and justice were greater than purity, and for this he was killed. I want to live like this. But I do not know if I am strong enough, or courageous enough. I know I will need your help to do this. I hope we stick together no matter what happens tomorrow.

Mary of Nazareth

HE WAS ALWAYS SO full of life. Even before he was born, he was full of life. He kept me awake at night. He made Joseph laugh with his kicking and wiggling. He was known as Yeshua of Nazareth, but actually he was Yeshua of Bethlehem, not too far to the south of here. Bethlehem is my hometown. That is where I met Joseph. That is where Yeshua was born. That is where so much happened. Maybe you have heard stories about those days. There were many rumors. I cannot explain. None of you would believe me. We had to leave shortly after he was born. We fled to Egypt and stayed there for two years. Joseph had dreams—it was so confusing, so threatening. I felt like we were constantly being pursued, chased. When we returned to Israel, we decided to go to Nazareth, where Joseph had some relatives. That was when we met Hassan, who guided us north and stayed with us. He was, is a blessing. The years in Nazareth were the best years. We no longer felt like we were being pursued. We were able to settle down, to live a normal life as our family grew. We made so many friends and had the support of family around us. I even thought that Yeshua might one day marry like his younger brothers and sisters. He was always so good with children. They would flock to him. Hassan tried very hard to place young women in his path. Ruth was our favorite—poor Ruth. She was so sad when he did not choose her. But he had made up his mind not to marry. Now we know why. Any wife would now be a widow. Any children would be fatherless. Somehow, I think he knew his life would be short. When he left Nazareth for Capernaum, I knew that once again he was being pursued. Adonai had singled him out like he had chosen those prophets of old—so I am not surprised that his life ended here in Jerusalem.

I am so grateful that all of you are here. We have gone through much together. My pain, my loss is also yours. Sometimes I tried to dissuade him, to turn him from the path he had chosen. After all, I was his mother. Of course, it was fruitless. You know him—how stubborn he could be—he got that from his father. In one way, I am glad Joseph is not here to know the pain. Sometimes I wish I were not here. I could not bear this alone. I do not know what the rest of you will do. I suppose some of you will continue his work, his preaching and teaching and healing. Some may go back to farming or fishing. I will go back to Nazareth. Shalomie, my dearest friend, has invited me to come live with her. I will always be a mother and a grandmother. I know I will be able to live with the fact that my eldest son died on a cross, like a criminal. No matter what anyone says, I will never be ashamed of him. Somehow, I believe his message will not die with him. Look at all of us! Look at the many poor and oppressed to whom he gave hope and a voice! He couldn't help himself. He was incorrigible. Even on the cross, as he was dying, he told that one thief next to him, "Today, you will be with me in Paradise." I almost laughed until I realized he meant it. His faith never wavered. His love of all people, even his killers, never waned. I will go back to Nazareth and try to do the same.

The last thing I have to do is to give this small chest of myrrh to you women. I have kept it for thirty years. It was a gift at his birth in Bethlehem. I have saved it for anointing him at his burial. Even then, long ago, I somehow knew he would die young. Please do not forget to take it with you in the morning. Now I need to get some sleep. Tomorrow is an important day.

Saturday Night and Beyond

Barabbas

IF I WEREN'T SO drunk, I would go out again in the dark and find some more Romans to kill. So far, we have only done two. One was a soldier who went down the wrong alley. The other was some rich guy whose purse is now paying for this lousy wine. After I was released from prison, I laid low for a day because I knew the Romans would follow me. I found some old friends and slept for a long time. At least I tried to sleep. I kept having this nightmare that I was back in prison, or on my way to a cross. I kept seeing this poor guy who was taken in my place. I would wake up in a sweat and cry out—I didn't even know his name. He was sure unpopular with the crowd who kept calling out my name. Why me? I wondered. Why I was so lucky? I would love to get Pilate alone somewhere. I would beat him real bad. Well, after a day of trying to sleep and fun with a few old whores, I thought I would get revenge on the Romans. Now I have drunk too much wine and I better just sleep it off.

Earlier this evening, I learned where they had buried the poor guy who had been crucified in my place. I wondered about him: who he was, where he came from, what he had done? I grabbed Micah and said we were going to this garden to find a tomb. He said nothing, which was his usual response. We snuck through the back alleys and found our way to this garden owned by some rich guy—Joseph something. When we got there, we were surprised to find a couple of the Temple guards on watch. What did they think? Like he was going to pop out of the tomb? Or maybe someone was going to steal his body and then tell everyone that he was alive again. I thought to myself, that's not a bad idea. We should steal his body and spread the rumor that he was alive. That would shake up Pilate and those religious folks. We would probably have to kill the guards, and that might be risky. Micah and I could move that big stone in front of the tomb. That's not the problem. Anyway, who cares what happens to him. I am just glad to be alive. I told Micah that if anything happened to me, I wanted to be buried in a tomb like that. We laughed and then just left.

We went back to his sister's house, where there were some new people drinking our wine. One of them was this big guy from Galilee. He said he worked for Annas, the high priest. He said I owed him my life. He said he was one of those hired to stir up the crowd and get me released and the other guy, this Rabbi Yeshua, crucified. I told him I wouldn't charge him for the wine. Then I asked him who this Rabbi was and why the high priest was out to get him. He told me he was hired because he was from Galilee and knew about the Rabbi from Capernaum. He laughed and called him "The Good Rabbi, the miracle worker, the lover of the rabble." He said he was some Galilean who got too popular and was teaching some new ways, some crazy ways, like "love your enemies" and "the meek shall inherit the earth," Junk like that. I looked over at Micah's sister Deborah and said, "Are you my enemy? 'Cause then I could love you." She smacked me. We all laughed. And then were silent. The big man went on: "So, when the Rabbi came to Jerusalem, he tore up the Temple and threw out the money changers and merchants. Annas did not take kindly to a loss of income. But they were afraid to arrest him publicly because he was so popular—everyone thought he was a prophet. I knew some of his disciples, so Annas asked me which one could be turned against him. I picked Judas because he was the most ambitious and liked nice tunics. He was also the one who was eager to make this Rabbi into some Messiah, some 'King of the Jews.' I guess you didn't see that sign they put on his cross, one of Pilate's jokes, 'Yeshua of Nazareth—King of the Jews.'" We all laughed and drank some more wine. He continued, "So, it was Judas who handed him over to the Temple guards on Thursday night. I hear they paid him thirty pieces of silver—that's more than I got for a lot more work. Anyway, he is dead and buried, but his disciples are still in Jerusalem. They think they are safe and in hiding, but everyone knows where they are. If I were them, I'd be heading for Galilee, and soon."

I thought to myself: what if I went and found some of his disciples? What would I ask them? Would they even talk to me? They would probably want me to say how sorry I was—well, I'm not! And what about this "love your enemies" crap? How does that work? I would want to know why they followed him. What did they see in him that was so special? I would ask them if they wanted revenge on Pilate and the Sanhedrin, Annas and Caiaphas and the rest. If they did, I would volunteer to help them. I could cut a few more throats. They probably would say something pious like, "No thank you. We forgive them." What a bunch of losers. Still, I am troubled because I deserved what I was about to get. I didn't deserve to be set free. Was it just plain luck? Or what? I wish I could believe what this Rabbi was telling everyone. Mercy? Love? Forgiveness? Where would that get me? All this makes my head hurt. Or maybe it is just the lousy wine.

Joel the Gardener

IT WAS JUST GETTING light when I got to the garden. The two Temple guards were asleep, so I tried to be quiet. I found my tools where I had left them yesterday. As it became lighter, I noticed that the stone that was supposed to seal the tomb was off to one side. I thought to myself, "I guess they are waiting for the ritual anointing and shrouding before they seal it for good." As I went off to another part of the garden, some women were coming down the path. A few moments later, I heard someone cry out. Then two of the women ran past me and out of the garden, back toward Jerusalem. They were clearly terrified. I thought maybe they woke the guards and were afraid of them. I just kept working on some trees that needed to be trimmed and then fertilized. A short time later two men came running into the garden, heading for Joseph's tomb. Soon they both came walking back, shaking their heads. I heard them talking: "Who could have rolled away the stone? Who would steal the Rabbi's body? Where could it be? Why would someone do this? What will we tell his mother?" They left the garden and then I became curious. I was aware of a strange light coming from the direction of the tomb and assumed that it was the sun reflecting off of something. But what was it?

I crept back to the tomb. The Temple guards had left, so something else must have frightened those women. The only person there was another woman, and she was weeping. She was crying to herself, "Where have they taken him? What have they done with him? All that is left are some burial clothes. Why? Why?" I was about to come closer, when I heard a voice. It was a man's voice, but a very quiet one. The woman did not look up. He said to her, "Woman. Why are you weeping? Who are you looking for?" She kept crying, and then said, "If you have taken his body away, just tell me where you have placed it and I will come and take him away." Then the man said, "Mary!" She looked up. She knew who was calling to her. I could see her face. She was both frightened and stunned. Then she smiled and wiped her tears and cried out, "Rabbouni!" She stood up and ran to embrace him, but he backed away. He held up his hand, which had a terrible scar in the middle, and said to her, "Do not cling to me! I must first return to Adonai. Soon I will come to be with you all again. Now, tell my sisters and brothers what you have seen. Tell them that I am returning to Adonai, the father of us all. Bring them my blessing of peace!" And then he was gone. The woman turned and walked out of the garden. She had this intense smile on her face, and she kept repeating the words, "I have seen the Lord! I have seen the Lord!"

When she had gone, I slowly crept up to the opening of the tomb and looked in. I admit I was frightened. I did not know what I would find. It was empty. At least it was empty of anyone's body. In one corner there was a linen shroud. There was a smaller linen cloth rolled up and tossed in a corner. Strangely enough, it did not smell of death. While I was wondering about all of this, I heard a rustle of feathers outside. I lowered my head and went out through the entrance. I looked up, expecting to see a hawk or an eagle. The sky was empty and there was nothing perched in any trees nearby. I was sure that I had heard a surge of wings. But then, this has been a strange morning so far. Weeping women! A mysterious man! An empty tomb! What's next?

Thomas of Sepphoris

OF COURSE, WE DIDN'T believe her. It was preposterous. Rabbi Yeshua—alive? It was easy for me to disbelieve. I am the most skeptical of all the disciples. I thought surely that some would believe Mary's story. "I have seen the Lord!" she cried as she came in the door. The other two women were still shaken and upset, but they simply said that the stone had been rolled away and that Rabbi Yeshua's body was gone. They said nothing about a resurrection. They were just frightened and frustrated because they could not properly anoint his body. Simon and John had also gone running to the tomb and confirmed what the two women had told us. We all thought that Mary was being hysterical. Someone even called it an idle tale, as if she so strongly wanted him to be alive that she was seeing things. Yet, Mary insisted she had seen and spoken to Rabbi. She said that he told her to tell the rest of us he was alive again. I wish it were true, but we all saw him carried from the cross to the tomb and placed inside. We even saw them roll the stone in front of the opening. Alive? Impossible! At least that is what I thought for a whole week.

The evening after Mary told us she had witnessed Rabbi Yeshua alive, I was feeling anxious and cramped, so I left the upper room and went to Bethany to visit some friends. They were neighbors of Mary and Martha and Lazarus. I said nothing about what Mary Magdalene was claiming. After what had happened with Lazarus, it might seem like a cruel joke. We had dinner, and I told them about Judas and his father and about how frightened we all were of the Romans. I did tell them that the women had gone to the tomb that morning and found it empty, and that we all assumed someone had taken Rabbi's body during the night. We had no idea why. And, so far, we had no idea where it was. His mother Mary was the most upset since she had saved this precious container of myrrh since his birth. She had wanted it used for anointing him in the tomb, and now all it would do would remind her of his death and the loss of his body. After dinner, I returned to Jerusalem. I knocked on the door, which I knew would be locked. I whispered my name, and someone opened the door. I was greeted by shouts of amazement and what I could only name as joy. Joy? I could not imagine why there was so much joy and laughter in the room.

Simon came and grabbed me and picked me off the ground saying, "He was here! He is alive! Mary was telling the truth! It's amazing, but true! He is alive!" When he put me down, I looked at the others and they all nodded. James told me how they were all in the locked room and no one was talking. He said, "Suddenly, out of nowhere, Rabbi Yeshua appeared, and said, 'Peace be with you!' John fell off of his chair, Shalomie screamed, Bartholomew almost jumped out of the window. We all stood up with our mouths open. Finally, Thaddeus asked, 'Is it you? Is it really you?' And Rabbi said, 'Yes. It is. I am risen.'" They all spoke at once, telling me what they asked and what he said, and I couldn't believe it all. I said to stop. Then I said that I would believe it only when I could see him for myself. I wanted to touch him, to put my fingers in the nail holes and feel the wound in his side.

A whole week had gone by and I was still unconvinced. We were all together again in that upper room. Again, the door was locked. Suddenly, out of nowhere, Rabbi Yeshua appeared and said, "Peace be with you!" This time, no one said a word. He looked at me and held out his hands. He said, "Thomas, come and touch my wounds. Put your hand in my side and in the nail holes in my hands. Do not be faithless but believing." I froze. Then I slowly moved to him and reached out my hand and put a finger in the hole in his hand, feeling the dried blood. I needed blood to tell me the truth. Then I placed my hand in his side and could feel his pulse, and the warmth of his body, his flesh. I looked into his face and saw, not disappointment, but compassion. I was the one who felt the disappointment, even shame. I fell to my knees and grasped his feet, and said, "My Lord and my God!" He raised me up and said, "Thomas, you now believe because you have seen. Blessed are and will be those who have not seen, but believe." Then he called all the disciples together around me. He spoke: "Last week I breathed on all of you with the breath of Adonai. I gave to you all the gift of the Holy Spirit: to forgive the sins of any, and to retain the sins of any. Now I give to Thomas this same power, this same gift." He took my head in his hands and breathed into my eyes. Still holding my head, he looked at me and told me I would travel far away for the sake of the gospel, and would suffer much, but would create a beloved community who would bear my name.

After that night, we would see him several more times. He would remind us of his teachings and of the gifts of love and compassion, of mercy and truth that Adonai has entrusted to us all. We continued to meet and to share stories. We also began to share our new and preposterous story with the people we met. Some just laughed; some walked away shaking their heads; others wanted to hear more; others came to believe in the love of Adonai through Rabbi Yeshua's life, death and resurrection. Someday someone will have to write down all these stories and words and memories. When they do, they will find that there will be more books than the world can hold. Until that time, we will continue to tell the story of the good news. And when people don't get it, we will simply tell it again—and again—and again. I know how to be stubborn.

Anna—A Servant in Emmaus

THAT VOICE! I WOULD recognize it anywhere. But how can that be? He is dead. Crucified. But that voice from the other room is his. I know it. I first heard it at the market near the city gate. He was teaching to crowds of people. He was warning them to beware of false teachers and to be honest in their repentance. He told them to be humble in their prayers and not pray with many words, but in the privacy of their closets. He said we are not to look for praise because we are pious or think of ourselves as better than others. He told a story about two men who went into the Temple to pray. One was a very religious man who prayed aloud to Adonai, listing all the good and righteous things he had done, and thanking Adonai that he was not like others, especially like the other man, who was a public sinner. The other man would not even look up to heaven, but beat his breast and told Adonai what a sinful person he was. He simply asked for forgiveness. Then, this Rabbi said something remarkable: "I tell you this sinful man, not the other one, went away to his house reconciled with Adonai. Truly, truly I tell you, the first will be last and the last first." Then he looked up and saw me listening. I felt his gaze go deeply into my soul; somehow, he knew my innermost fears and longings. Yet, I did not feel shame, rather I felt loved and renewed.

This morning my master had gone into Jerusalem with a friend. They had both become followers of the Rabbi from Capernaum. They were present when he caused the riot in the Temple and then listened to his preaching and watched him heal many in the city. They came to believe that he was the coming one, the Messiah who would restore Israel to greatness. Their hopes were crushed when he was crucified a few days ago. My master was furious that the leaders of the Sanhedrin had handed him over to the Romans who had killed him. They had gone to be with the other disciples and to share in the grief. I was alone with my baking of bread and cleaning the house. I assumed they would be back for supper, so I was preparing a lamb stew with leeks and garlic.

It was almost dark when they returned. They had a guest with them. They sat down at the table and talked. That was when I heard his voice. I dared not look into the other room for fear that I was wrong. I listened closely to their talk about an empty tomb, a vision of angels, insistent women, and hope against hope. I could not wait any longer so I brought wine to the table, three cups. When I looked at him, he smiled and there was light all around him. My master and his friend did not see it. I am sure they did not see it. I returned to the kitchen. I could hardly breathe, and my hands were shaking as I reached for the warm loaf of bread. I placed the loaf on a tray and slowly walked back into the dining room. I placed it on the table. He took it in his hands. I could see the scars. I turned toward the kitchen as he blessed and broke the bread. I did not want him to see my tears. A few minutes later, my master came running into the kitchen shouting, "It was him! It was him! He is alive! We must tell the others. We are returning to Jerusalem." And they left me alone, yet not alone. I cleared the table and daringly ate some bread and drank some wine with my heart pounding and my eyes wide open.

Mary of Nazareth

I AM BACK IN Nazareth. Shalomie and her husband have provided me with a small guest room in their home. I am fortunate to be near my children and grandchildren again, although I have become a famous, maybe infamous, person. I remember Yeshua once said that a prophet is usually without honor in his own country—true also for the prophet's mother. Many people just do not know what to say or what to ask me about. Most everyone has been friendly and helpful. Even the rabbi of the synagogue has come to visit to talk about what he calls my "adventure." He asked that we not talk about Yeshua and the disciples and the events in Jerusalem. I said that would be fine with me, since there are so many more who want to talk about nothing else. Hassan has become very protective of me. He was a great help in bringing the few things left at the house in Capernaum. He keeps telling me I need to rest and focus on my family. His wife, Rachel, has become a close friend. My head still spins when I think of the last few weeks.

We stayed in Jerusalem for several weeks after Yeshua's "re-birth." He appeared to the disciples and many others and spent time teaching and encouraging them to be bold and outspoken about the new world of hope and salvation. It took me many days to figure out who I was. I was still his mother, but our relationship was all changed and different. I am still confused about it. I will just have to trust in Adonai, as he says. And I do. After all, it was Adonai who brought my son back to life. Who wouldn't trust in such power and love? Then, one day, he told the disciples and followers that it was time for him to return to Adonai. They were now the leaders of the new Israel, the new creation, the new world of faith, hope and love that will sweep the world. They were his witnesses to the whole world. He kept emphasizing the mission to the "whole world." It seemed impossible, but then so did resurrection once seem impossible. One day we all went to the Mount of Olives and he asked us to look out as far as we could into the distance and to imagine traveling to faraway places with the good news of peace and hope and love. We stood and looked out. And when we turned around, he was gone. That was the last we saw of him—my son, my first-born, my rabbi, my gift to the world, the whole world.

Before all of this happened, I wanted to return to Bethlehem, to visit my home and the birthplace of Yeshua. Shalomie and several of the women and disciples went with me. It is not a long walk, and I was very excited to see if the village had changed much. We found my old family home, and the marketplace was almost the same. We found the house that Joseph and I had lived in for not even a year. It had been enlarged and there were several small children playing in front of the door. I have to admit that I got home-sick. I was tempted to try to find some cousins, but decided not to look for anyone from my past. I felt dizzy when I recalled that night that I heard the voice of Adonai's angel asking me to be Yeshua's mother. I could have said, "No," I suppose. But I didn't. I said, "Yes!" and my whole life, my entire world was changed. I began to cry as I remembered how tender and caring Joseph was when I told him. He, too, could have said, "No." But he didn't. He loved me. He trusted me. I miss him very much. I recalled Yeshua's first cries, his first words, his first steps, his first girlfriend, even his first miracle. I remember his first sermon. We had just moved to Capernaum, and he was to preach in the synagogue. He spoke of repentance. He was always so dramatic. He said that the word actually meant to be walking in one direc-tion, and he stepped down the aisle, and then to turn and walk in another direction, and he quickly turned and went back to stand in front of the ark. He said that repentance is not just a feeling or an emotion, it was something visible, a change that other people could see. He also said that repentance was not a burden, and then he bent over as if with a great weight on his shoulders. Then he stood up straight and smiled. For him repentance was an unburdening, a joy, a release. I still remember that.

We returned to Jerusalem in time for the festival of Shavuot. There were people from many faraway places, some as distant as Rome and Africa. It was strange, walking through the streets and hearing so many different languages being spoken and shouted. The streets were full of people dressed in exotic tunics and robes and dresses. The many colors were beautiful to-gether, as were the smells of spices and incense. I had never before seen so many different people in one place. Maybe that was the point. Since we had been charged with preaching our message to the whole world, it was only right that the whole world had come to us. This all came true on the day of

Shavuot. We were on our way to the Temple when a hot, dry wind blew in from the hills, and everyone became quiet. Then what looked like tongues of fire hovered over all the disciples and followers, making the winds even hotter. Then Simon stood up in the Court of the Gentiles and began to preach about Rabbi Yeshua's life and death and resurrection. He spoke in our language, Aramaic, but everyone from all the faraway places seemed to understand what he was saying. People were shocked and confused because they knew we were all Galileans. Someone shouted, "They are all drunk!" and some others laughed. When Simon was finished, many people asked about this new message and what it meant. We had a lot of explaining to do and spent the rest of the day talking about our good news. Many came to have faith and then were baptized.

My place is now in Nazareth. I have done my part. I will continue to pray and to share my story with any who wish to hear it. I will tell them about my visions and the voices and the mysterious yet very real birth. I will tell of the shepherds and the startling appearance of the three Magi and their expensive gifts. I will tell of our flight into Egypt and escape from Herod. I will tell of coming to Nazareth and raising our family, of Joseph's love and work, and his untimely death. And I will tell of my son, Yeshua: his miracles, his healings, his words of love and compassion for all. Last, I will tell of his death and resurrection, and his promise of peace to a violent world. Then I will show the container of myrrh that I have saved since his birth. I will say that this was intended for Yeshua's burial—and now it is for the healing of the world. I will open the jar and have people smell how sweet the aroma of peace. Sometimes, some disciples will come to Nazareth to visit. They always try to convince me to come with them, to travel to faraway places, to spread the word. I simply say, "No. You go! I will stay. You go! I will stay."

Glossary

Adonai

A Hebrew word generally translated as "Lord." Since, in Jewish practice, the four-letter name of "God" was not to be spoken, when it appeared in a text of Hebrew Scriptures, the reader substituted "Adonai," The title "Lord" was also one of the earliest divine titles given to Jesus (cf. 1 Cor. 12:3; John 20:18, 28.)

Annas

Appointed by Quirinius, the Roman legate to Syria, in 6 CE, he became the first High Priest in the newly formed Roman province of Judaea. He served with his son, Caiaphas, for several decades. He was part of Jesus' trial (John 18:19–24) and also of Peter and John (Acts 4:1–22).

Anathoth

A small village about 3 miles north of Jerusalem, belonging to the tribe of Benjamin. It was the home of Jeremiah the prophet and was one of the cities of refuge (Joshua 21:18).

Beelzebul

The name of a major demon, derived from a Philistine deity, Ba'al.

Bethany

A village one mile southeast of Jerusalem, close to the Mount of Olives; the home of Mary, Martha, Lazarus, and Simon the Leper.

Bethphage

A village next to Bethany on the Mount of Olives.

Boanerges

An Aramaic term usually translated "Sons of Thunder;" the nickname of James and John.

Caesarea

Sometimes referred to as Caesarea Maritima, it was a port city south of Haifa, built by Herod the Great in 27 BCE and dedicated to the Roman Emperor. It served as an administrative center for the province of Judaea and was probably home to Pilate when he was Governor.

Caesarea Philippi

Located just below Mt. Hermon in the Golan Heights, built on the site of an ancient shrine to the Canaanite god Ba'al, later dedicated to the Roman god Pan, the city was then rebuilt by Herod the Great and dedicated to Caesar. The name Philippi was added when Herod's son, Phillip, became tetrarch of the area east of Galilee, now southern Syria.

Caiaphas

His full name is Joseph son of Caiaphas. He was the son-in-law of Annas and served as High Priest from 18 to 36 CE. He figures prominently in the trial of Jesus and is mentioned extensively by 1st Century Jewish historian Josephus.

Capernaum

A village on the northwestern shore of the Sea of Galilee. It figured as the focal point of Jesus' ministry and was the home of several disciples.

Court of the Gentiles

The Temple in Jerusalem was greatly reconstructed by Herod the Great (37 BCE–4 CE). Surrounding the actual Temple and the Court of the Women, the Court of the Gentiles was a large open space for all the residents and visitors to Jerusalem.

Decapolis

Literally "Ten Cities," a loose federation of cities, including Damascus (in Syria) and Philadelphia (modern day Amman, capital of Jordan). They were an important coalition of Greek and Roman centers of trade and culture.

Essenes

A Jewish sect generally associated with the site of Qumran and the Dead Sea Scrolls. While the New Testament does not mention them, Josephus, the 1st Century Jewish historian, describes the Essenes as a group dedicated to ritual purity and an ascetic life of separation. They flourished from 200 BCE to 100 CE. Some scholars speculate that John the Baptist might have been a member of this sect.

Frankincense

A hardened, gum-like resin from the Boswellia Sacra tree that is used as incense and perfume, as well as in medicines. Because it is so rare, it remains very expensive.

Gennesaret

One of several names for the Sea of Galilee.

Herod

The Roman appointed king of Judaea 37 BCE–4 CE, frequently surnamed "the Great." Although of Arab origin from southern Palestine, he was a practicing Jew. He is best known as a builder of aqueducts, fortresses, and the Second Temple. His personal life was filled with suspicion, mistrust, and violence: he had 8–10 wives and 14 children, many of whom he had murdered.

Herod Antipas

Son of Herod the Great, 20 BCE–39 CE, he ruled as tetrarch of the regions of Galilee and Perea, respectively in the north and in the south of Palestine, across the Jordan River, east of the Dead Sea. In the New Testament, he was responsible for the death of John the Baptist.

Joppa

An ancient seaport on the Mediterranean, established 2500 BCE as a Canaanite city, later called Jaffa and now surrounded by Tel Aviv.

Kerioth

An ancient village 35 miles south of Jerusalem and 15 mile west of the Dead Sea, possibly the home of Judas Iscariot.

Machaereus

A palace fortified by Herod the Great, several miles east of the Dead Sea in the territory of the Nabateans, from which Herod's first wife came. This was one of three fortresses/palaces, including Masada and Herodium, that figured in the Jewish rebellion against Rome in 66–70 CE. According to 1st century Jewish historian Josephus, the site of the death of John the Baptist.

Magi

A title used for Zoroastrian priests from Persia. They were astronomers/astrologers as well as religious leaders and scholars.

Megiddo

The place name given to a plain in northern Palestine which runs from the Mediterranean coast east to the Jordan valley and is thus militarily strategic for controlling the north-south trade routes. It was the site of many significant battles between imperial forces from Egypt, Assyria, Babylon, and Persia. On the southern edge is a mountain (in Hebrew, *har*), hence the name "Armageddon," which has taken on mythical importance as the site of the final conflict between God and the forces of evil.

Messiah

A Hebrew term which means "anointed one" and is used to denote persons and objects that restore, liberate, or save the people of Israel. In the Dead Sea Scrolls, there appear to be two 'messiahs:' one religious and one political. In the New Testament, the Greek word for "messiah" is *christos*, which became the primary title for Jesus of Nazareth.

Glossary

Mt. Gerizim

In north central Israel and associated with the Patriarchs and early Israelite assemblies, it later became a holy place for Samaritans.

Myrrh

A gum resin harvested from various thorny trees found in the Arabian Peninsula, Somalia, and Ethiopia. It is used in perfume, incense, and medicines. It is highly valued and was traded widely in biblical times.

Nabateans

Originally a Bedouin people from the Arabian Peninsula who settled in the land east of the Jordan Valley, the Dead Sea, Edom, and southern Syria. Their capital was at Petra and they were rivals of Herod the Great.

Nain

A small rural village in Galilee, 6 mile south of Nazareth, mentioned in Luke 7:11–17.

Pharisees

A movement within Judaism that began during the Second Temple era (515 BCE–70 CE) composed of pious lay people and Scribes. They held not only to the written Torah but to the oral traditions, including the prophets, and promoted the synagogue as a local expression of Jewish life, study, and worship. They were 'progressive' in the sense that they relied on reason and sought to change Jewish practice to fit the historical context.

Petra

An ancient city of the Nabatean kingdom, dating to at least the 4th century BCE. Located in present day Jordan, 150 miles southeast of Jerusalem, Petra was on several important trade routes of the ancient near east and is now a popular tourist site.

Sadducees

Members of the priestly sect of traditional Judaism, they held only to the written text of the Torah and were this more 'conservative' than the Pharisees. By the time of Herod the Great, they had become a wealthy and aristocracy, maintaining good relations with the Romans. They upheld the centrality of worship in the Jerusalem Temple.

Sanhedrin

From the Greek word meaning "sitting together," hence an assembly. In the New Testament, the word probably refers to the Great Sanhedrin of Jerusalem. It comprised 71 sages or elders, sometimes including the high priest, and gathered to judge religious and civil cases. In smaller cities there were also Sanhedrins of smaller numbers who served as courts.

Sea of Kinneret

Another name for the Sea of Galilee

Sepphoris

This city was several miles northwest of Nazareth and served as the Roman administrative center for Galilee. Its name is derived from the Hebrew word *tzippor*, bird, since it was "perched like a bird on a high hill." Though not mentioned in the Bible, it had a significant Jewish population. It was destroyed during a rebellion but was rebuilt by Herod Antipas and remained supportive of Rome during the Jewish Rebellion of 66–70 CE.

Shavuot

Known in English as the Feast of Weeks or Pentecost, it is a Jewish festival which takes place 49 days—seven weeks—after Passover. It marks the first wheat harvest and the giving of the Torah on Mt. Sinai. It is one of three "Pilgrimage Festivals," hence the crowds in Jerusalem in Acts 2.

Sicarii

From the Latin *sicarius*, dagger-man, they were a small splinter group of Jewish Zealots, named for their use of *sicae*, a small dagger used to assassinate Romans and sympathizers in Zealot resistance prior to the Jewish Revolt of 66–70 CE.

Scribes

Their primary task was to copy the Hebrew Scriptures and to draw up legal documents (marriage, divorce, sale of property, etc.). Most villages had at least one Scribe. They also served in the Sanhedrin and helped interpret the Torah. In the New Testament, they often debate with Jesus and other rabbis.

Son of Man

A very controversial expression that occurs 81 times in the New Testament and only in the sayings of Jesus. It can refer to a future, coming figure, generally associated with judgment; or to a suffering figure (usually Jesus himself); or a present, working figure. One primary source of this title is Daniel 7:13–14, in which the 'person' is portrayed as a transcendent and powerful being who ushers in judgment and a new era. This figure became very popular in intertestamental writings (250 BCE–100 CE), especially in apocalyptic texts.

Tiberias

A city on the Sea of Galilee, founded by Herod Antipas in 20 CE and named for the Emperor, Tiberius. It was chosen because it was close to some hot springs popular with Roman settlers.

Torah

Literally, God's "guidance" or "instruction" for humans. When limited to the written form, it refers to the first five books of Moses in the Hebrew Scriptures. It can also include the Talmud, or oral Torah, which includes later Rabbinic writings and traditions.

Tyre

An ancient Phoenician port city, founded in 2700 BCE, and later was part of Egyptian, Greek and Roman empires. It was located just north of the border of Israel, so in a Gentile region. It was known as the home of Jezebel, the wife of King Ahab, and thus became a symbol of contention with Jewish worship and practice.

Valley of Hinnom

In Hebrew "Gehenna," located to the southeast of the old city of Jerusalem, it became a place for the burial of the poor and those deemed unworthy of a religious burial. Also associated with the fires used to burn rubbish from the city, the word "Gehenna" became associated with hell or a place of punishment.

Zealots

A Jewish sect identified by the historian Josephus as a militant, violent resistance to Roman occupation of Israel. It is sometimes associated with the *sicarii*, and with the Jewish nationalism that led to the revolt of 66–70 CE, ending at Masada when a thousand defenders took their own lives rather than surrender.

CPSIA information can be obtained
at www.ICGtesting.com
Printed in the USA
LVHW040342290322
714673LV00012B/620